CLASS OF JUNE-1921.
P.S. 134 BROOKLYN, N.Y.

I REMEMBER BROOKLYN

Memories From Famous Sons and Daughters

RALPH MONTI

A BIRCH LANE PRESS BOOK PUBLISHED BY CAROL PUBLISHING GROUP

A Birch Lane Press Book
Published by Carol Publishing Group
Birch Lane Press is a registered
trademark of Carol Communications, Inc.

Editorial Offices
600 Madison Avenue
New York, NY 10022

Sales & Distribution Offices
120 Enterprise Avenue
Secaucus, NJ 07094

In Canada: Musson Book Company
A division of General Publishing Co.
Unlimited Don Mills, Ontario

Book design: Morris Taub

Manufactured in the United States
of America
10 9 8 7 6 5 4 3 2 1

Carol Publishing Group books are
available at special discounts for bulk
purchases, for sales promotions, fund
raising, or educational purposes. Special
editions can be created to specifications.
For details contact: Special Sales
Department, Carol Publishing Group,
120 Enterprise Avenue, Secaucus, N.J.
07094

**Library of Congress Cataloging-in-
Publication Data**

Monti, Ralph,
    I remember Brooklyn : memories
of favorite sons and daughters / by
Ralph Monti.
      p.   cm.
    "A Birch Lane Press book."
    ISBN 1-55972-093-X
    1. Brooklyn (New York, N.Y.)—
Biography. 2. Brooklyn (New York,
N.Y.)—Social life and customs. 3.
New York (N.Y.)—Biography. 4.
New York (N.Y.)—Social life and
customs 5. Celebrities—New York
(N.Y.)—Biography. I. Title.
F129.B7M66 1991
974.7'23'0092—dc20   91-22830
    [B]   CIP

ACKNOWLEDGMENTS

I wish to thank the staff librarians at the Central Research Library and The Performing Arts Research Center of the New York Public Library for their invaluable assistance, especially Ms. Ruth Carr and her fine staff at the U.S. History, Local History & Genealogy division. I am indebted to Professor John Manbeck of Kingsborough Community College for allowing me access to his Kingsborough Historical Society collection.

For their advice, encouragement and friendship, thanks to Gina and Murray Becker, Nick Di Martino, Bob Greenman, Howard Morhaim, Jean-Daniel Noland, Ed Sokol, Teresa Stacy, Steve and Barbara Zammarchi. A special thank you to Anna and Alan Marcus for all their support. To my editor, Carole Stuart, for her suggestions that made the final manuscript that much better, and to Morris Taub who has executed a wonderful book design.

I also wish to thank the booking agents, secretaries, personal assistants, and publicity people who helped coordinate the interview sessions. And, of course, to the illustrious Brooklynites, whose memories appear herein, for taking the time to speak with me about their days in Brooklyn.

And to my wife, Margaret, whose precious love and support makes all my efforts worthwhile.

To my parents, Guy and Marianna Monti

C O N T E N T S

What memories do you have of growing up in Brooklyn? Perhaps it's a warm summer evening sitting out on the stoop. The smell of a sizzling hot dog being scorched on a Coney Island griddle. The excited roar of an Ebbets Field crowd as the Dodgers take the field. The Saturday morning hustle and bustle on Fulton Street. The trolley ride over the Manhattan Bridge. The wisecracking candy-store man down the street. The luscious taste of a chocolate egg cream. The endless games of stickball. The open-air concerts at Manhattan Beach. The Sunday afternoon walk in Prospect Park. Do any of these memories ring your Brooklyn memory bell?

Webster's defines a memory as "a person, thing, happening, or act remembered." Understandably, because it doesn't take into account memories that are from Brooklyn, the definition is short, boring, and to the point. But suppose we made up our own entry, one that would expand the definition. What if we asked the folks at Webster's to describe a *Brooklyn* memory. Could they come up with a suitable definition? Offer a description that captured the essence of that memory? Give the world an accurate description of what Brooklynites feel inside when they reflect about their times in Brooklyn? Consider the following:

Brook-lyn mem-o-ry *n*, *pl* **-ies**
1 : a person, thing, happen-

ing, or act remembered that makes a person excited, nostalgic, and passionate **2** : a memory that causes a person to break out into song, dance with glee, or jump from his seat **3** : a recollection that instills pride and inspires a person to beat his chest and sing hosannas to his past **4** : a remembrance that is cherished and passed on to generations of children and grandchildren with unreserved affection **5** : a memory that consumes the spirit.

Would these do it? Do these definitions capture the essence of a Brooklyn memory? It's close, you say? What, some of you argue, it still ain't no cigar? Well, perhaps you're right.

Several years ago, as I was walking along Ocean Parkway, under a night of twinkling stars and a shimmering full moon (okay, so I'm romanticizing here a bit), I was struck with the notion that a book loaded with Brooklyn memories would be a grand idea. I could tell the world, through a collection of memories, how fascinating a place Brooklyn truly is. Having lived there for many years myself, I was moved by its rich tradition, its natural and architectural landscape, its incredibly diverse people, and its important place in New York and American history. Unquestionably I considered Brooklyn the greatest place on earth. Motivated by this fascination, I read practically everything there was to read

about Brooklyn, yet the one thing I found lacking was a book that described Brooklyn through its greatest resource: its people. I decided that one day my memory book would be that book. I would tell the Brooklyn story through the eyes, ears, nose, touch, and taste of its people.

During the planning stages of the book, I decided that if I needed to speak with people from Brooklyn, why not its most fascinating sons and daughters? Why not men and women who, through good old-fashioned Brooklyn enterprise, have distinguished themselves in the arts, sciences, business and political worlds? I already knew that the universe of eminent Brooklynites was substantial and their contributions to the world could fill a volume of *Who's Who in America*. It was the matter of getting in touch with these people that would be key to the success of the book.

As I began my journey through a hectic maze of publicists, personal managers, daily schedulers, and secretaries, it soon became obvious that I had touched a sensitive chord. The very mention of the *B* word opened doors. Although most had long ago moved away from Brooklyn, they all still loved the place and were eager to answer my questions about their memories: What was it like for them to grow up there? What did they remember about the houses or apartments they grew up in? What was their neighborhood like? How do they remember their family, neighbors, teachers, and childhood friends? What

sights and sounds did they remember most? What was their favorite activity in Brooklyn? How did they remember Brooklyn during the Depression and World War II? What are their favorite memories about Coney Island? Prospect Park? The Brooklyn Dodgers? The Brooklyn Botanic Garden? The Navy Yard? Were they a street kid or a bookworm? An athlete or klutz? Prim and proper or a tomboy? They eagerly answered these questions and more.

Because I wanted them to have fun as they focused on their growing-up days in Brooklyn, I made it a point not to bring up present business. Any discussion about an upcoming movie, album, book, concert date, political campaign, or business decision was shelved. I wanted to talk to these people as dyed-in-the-wood Brooklynites and not as present-day celebrities. As we talked about their days in Brooklyn, the discussions evolved into longer sessions than the original time scheduled (many got so wrapped up with their memories that our talks averaged over two hours). Many echoed similar sentiments: How proud they were to be from Brooklyn. What a one-of-a-kind place Brooklyn is. Why they lamented for their children, who, despite having a better material life, would never experience the flavor of growing up in such a special place. How, despite their "moving up" in the world, some to such elegant addresses as Beverly Hills or Fifth Avenue, they still missed the old neighborhood and the people they knew there.

And finally, how *lucky* they were to be born or raised in Brooklyn. *Lucky* was the theme word I heard most often. That in spite of the hardships they endured and the poverty and despair many of them experienced there, most looked back on their Brooklyn days as their luckiest days. Brooklyn was the place that shaped their personalities and taught them how to survive, compete, and succeed.

To my secret glee, some grew so passionate as they discussed their Brooklyn memories, they excitedly jumped from their seats to act out a childhood memory. Others broke out into a school song or sang a favorite tune they used to sing on a street corner. Some told secret tales of adolescent love tribulations or troubling childhood insecurities. Interwoven among their memories were fond tales of loving parents, a favorite uncle or aunt, the caring teacher, the close childhood friendships, the crazy schoolyard antics, the Saturday morning movie-house trips, the summer evenings spent playing in the street, the loud stickball and stoopball games, the exciting Coney Island excursions, the block parties and holiday parades—memories all bound with a Brooklyn thread.

The celebrities that are presented here, of course, do not make up the total number that call Brooklyn their home. Because of schedule conflicts, there were some who could not accommodate my request for an interview. We will perhaps save their memories for another volume. To further broaden the book's scope, I have supplemented the interviews with excerpts from autobiographies of celebrities recalling their Brooklyn days. While some of these passages were written by people who have since passed on, their recollections of Brooklyn remain just as fresh and exciting.

As you read the memories that are presented here, you'll undoubtedly sense a certain Brooklyn karma. For those of us who have been fortunate to have lived (or live) in Brooklyn, it's a shared spirit that'll never let go. Indeed, once you've been infected by the Brooklyn charm, it will last a lifetime. When Gertrude Stein was asked to describe the city of Oakland, she offered up her legendary "There's no *there*, there" quip. Maybe, if she had taken a train east and gotten off in Brooklyn, she might have been remembered for saying, "There's a helluva lot of *there*, there." Indeed there is, was, and always will be.

—Ralph Monti
Fall 1991

A

B R O O K L Y N

H I G H

S C H O O L

F I G H T   S O N G

B is for the beach in Coney Island,
R is for the oRange when it peels,
O is for the O in Ocean Parkway, just put the other
O in Ebbets Field!
K and
L mean absolutely nothing,
Y and
N are always in the way!

J O E Y

Comedian and newspaper columnist

The 1920s was a time when many

Brooklyn neighborhoods were inhabited by the so-called tough

guys. These neighborhood gangsters were involved in all kinds

of illegal activities, yet the irony of it was that many people in

the area, from the shoe repairman to the corner grocer, looked

A D A M S

to these guys for protection. Many of the thugs lived right up the

street with their families, so they kept an eye on things as far as

crime was concerned. If you lived on a street with a few of these

hoodlums around, chances are you didn't have to worry about

crime. One of those neighborhoods was Brownsville, the area

where I was born and raised. We lived at 96 Christopher Street, in a rented apartment that was a four-flight walk-up. My parents believed in being close. I mean real close: I was raised with three brothers, a sister, an aunt, and an uncle. Living quarters for the nine of us was three small rooms.

As many people know, Fiorello La Guardia, the great mayor of New York, took me under his wing when I was a young boy. His encouragement and support played a major part in my success. My career started with the Loews people. I was about sixteen or seventeen at the time and just breaking into show business, when I landed a job emceeing weekly amateur shows at the Loews Pitkin and Premier in Brooklyn. Though I got very little money, it was a chance for me to learn and polish my act. In addition to introducing the acts, I would do all kinds of comedy. There were dozens of entertainers who wanted to perform— dancers, violinists, comedians, singers, and a variety of vaudeville acts. Because they were paying me so little, Loews got the bright idea that, as an extra bonus, they would honor me with a parade. It would also help promote their theater business. So one sunny afternoon, the Joey Adams Parade strutted down Pitkin Avenue, honoring my work at their theaters. It was really quite a carnival and the neighborhood had a ball.

One occasion I'll never forget was a night during the Christmas season when I was feeling very lonely. I had just started working at Loews and still hadn't made a name for myself. I had few friends and things weren't going along as quickly as I'd wanted. Because it was the Christmas season, I decided to throw a party. One of the stagehands helped me set it up with the $4.50 I had in my pocket. We put out a really big spread and were very excited. Unfortunately, when party time came, nobody showed up. Not one! I was brokenhearted. I felt very alone. I went home feeling down. About five minutes to midnight the doorbell rang and when I opened the door, there were about thirty people outside asking where the party was. Standing right behind them was La Guardia. He had heard what happened, so he rounded up a bunch of people and came to my apartment. I ended up having a great time that evening and its wonderful memory I'll always cherish.

I always enjoyed entertaining, no matter where I was. La Guardia arranged it so that I could make extra money during the days, supplementing the very little income I was making with Loews in the evening. He got me a job in the hat department at Namm's Department Store in Brooklyn. The hat counter faced a daily stream of passersby on their way to various parts of the store. One day I suddenly got the urge to entertain the customers by telling jokes. I became an instant hit with my jokes, and soon hat sales rose. I called my department "Adam's Hats" and several of my coworkers called me "Ol' 6⅞." I had a ball working in Namm's Department Store.

When my father and mother emigrated from Russia, their name was Abramowitz, which was later changed to Abrams and then later to Adams. If the United States customs people didn't change your name, some-

where along the way you might do it yourself. It was not uncommon in those days. Many immigrants from Poland, Italy, Russia, Germany, and Scandinavia had names that were difficult to pronounce. The notion of Americanizing one's name wasn't any big deal, though it was looked down upon from some

quarters. This struck me the evening I was to star on the popular television show *Strike It Rich*. The CBS network had their top people in the studio, most of them milling about before airtime. A very tall, distinguished CBS executive walked over to me and introduced himself as Wendell Adams. Clearly he was not of recent immigrant stock.

"Mr. Adams," he said, "I've heard about you for several years now. I've seen you in the theaters and heard you on radio. You are truly one of my favorite performers. I was wondering, sir, if we might be related."

It was clear there could be no possible relation, but I decided to play along with this charade. So without missing a beat, I turned to him and answered: "We might, sir. What was your name before it was Adams?"

He looked at me with disdain and quickly turned away.

I've been attracted to the glamour of the

press box as far back as I can remember. Unlike most kids, when

I went to a Dodger, Knickerbocker, or Ranger game, I was less

intrigued by the players than by the sportswriters and

broadcasters as they covered the game. While other youngsters

M A R V

NBC-TV sportscaster

idolized Gil Hodges or Duke Snider, my heroes were Vin Scully

and Sam Goldaper. I was a consummate sports fanatic and

though I practically lived in the schoolyard at P.S. 195 in Man-

hattan Beach, I knew early on I was an average athlete. It didn't

take me long to realize that if I wanted to work in the sports world, it would be through skills as a journalist, rather than the perfection of my jump shot.

I began my journalism career with a Revere tape recorder my father bought for me. I'd spend countless evenings in my house on Kensington street calling a game off the television. My fictitious radio station, WMPA, was named after my initials. When I wasn't calling games off the TV, I'd do live broadcasts of Ping-Pong matches, which, you might imagine, is a tricky game to call. While I continued this obsession to sharpen my broadcast skills, I made my entry into

A L

the sports world through a summer job with the Brooklyn Dodgers. I was assigned a variety of jobs, from working the sports board and assisting in the ticket office, to running errands for the office executives. One of the great benefits of working for the Dodgers was getting two free tickets to each home game. I was particularly excited because the seats were located in the overhang section, adjacent to the Dodger broadcast booth. I was thrilled to be so close to Vin Scully as he called a game. Oftentimes, when Scully's

broadcast ended and everyone was gone, I'd wander into the broadcast booth and collect the commercial announcements that were strewn on the floor. Eventually I brought my tape recorder with me to the games, and I worked on my technique in the overhang. When I got a job as a ball boy for the New York Knicks, this practice continued at Madison Square Garden, calling games into my tape recorder for the Knickerbockers, Rangers, and college teams, too. By the time I did my first professional broadcast, I was well prepared.

B E

My sports fanaticism was tempered by piano and accordion lessons because my mother felt I should have a taste of culture. But she stretched the point when she enrolled me in tap lessons. I agonized over the hours my mother forced me to practice the piano, although I took solace in the fact my younger brothers were going through the same misery. Although I reached a level of proficiency where I was good enough to give recitals, as well as teach new students, my heart was never in it. There was, however,

some merit to the piano lessons. The trade-off was my piano teacher's mimeograph machine. I had recently started a fan club for the New York Knicks, so the machine was a godsend for me to publish *Knick Knacks*, the fan club's newsletter. I've always teased my mother about those piano lessons. Besides the accessibility they gave me to a mimeograph machine, the most fruitful results of my keyboard exercises were an increase in my typing speed and the ability of my now-stretched hand to palm a basketball.

Basket number one in the

R T

Manhattan Beach playground was the court where some of the best basketball talent in the country came to play their "schoolyard games." Players like Connie Hawkins, Doug Moe, Billy Cunningham, and Roger Brown are several notable players who played in Manhattan Beach. When the hotshots played a game, the playground would quickly fill with spectators, sometimes four to five people deep. Most of these guys came from other neighborhoods in Brooklyn, but somehow Manhattan Beach's basket number one

evolved into the meeting place for serious basketball. The better ballplayers would often be accompanied by an entourage, and it was amusing to see the contrast of the more flamboyant hangers-on mingling with the restrained and conservative residents of Manhattan Beach. The common denominator for all those watching, however, was the enthusiasm for great basketball.

Among my journalistic heroes, the person I idolized the most was Marty Glickman, the dean of New York sportscasters. I eventually went to work for Marty through my sports information activities at Abraham Lincoln High School. During my years at Lincoln, I stayed very busy. I wrote a column for *The Lincoln Log*, the school's newspaper, was the sports editor for the yearbook, the high-school correspondent for the New York newspapers, and wrote and published game programs for Lincoln's sporting events. I felt strongly that programs should be published for every game, so, using the school's facilities I'd print programs for the basketball and football games. Everyone, including the coaches, loved the programs, which included all the stats for the event, as well as pregame gossip. Marty had just begun his "High School Game of the Week" series, and one of his first games was a Lincoln-Madison contest.

When he arrived at the school, the coaches advised him to see me because I had compiled information and comprehensive statistics for the two teams. He was impressed with the data I collected and subsequently used my information for the broadcast. After the game, Glickman and the producer of the show, David Garth, who eventually went on to become an influential political consultant, hired me as their researcher for the remainder of the season. When I graduated from Syracuse University, I resumed working with Marty and Garth, as a producer for the "High School Game of the Week" series. Marty's generous encouragement during that time was a big influence on my broadcast career, and helped pave the way for Kensington Street's WMPA radio personality.

A HUGE BANNER AND CEREMONIAL BUNTING DRAPE BROOKLYN BOROUGH HALL AS FESTIVITIES TAKE PLACE ON DODGER VICTORY CELEBRATION DAY, SEPTEMBER 16, 1955. BOROUGH PRESIDENT JOHN CASHMORE PROCLAIMED THE DAY TO HONOR THE DODGERS' CLINCHING OF THE 1955 PENNANT.

Night was a wonderful time in Brooklyn in

the thirties, especially in warm weather. Everyone would be sit-

ting on their stoops, since air conditioning was unknown except

in movie houses, and so was television without exception. There

was nothing to keep one in the house. Furthermore, few people

Science-fiction author

ISAAC

owned automobiles, so there was nothing to carry one away. That

left the streets and the stoops, which were thus full, and the very

fullness served as an inhibition to street crime. People were

everywhere, talking, laughing, gossiping, and the roadways were

relatively empty. I would walk all over the neighborhood,

FOLLOWING PAGE: ORIGINALLY SETTLED BY DUTCH FARMERS IN THE EARLY 1600S, BROOKLYN TODAY ENCOMPASSES OVER 1,600 MILES OF STREETS. THE LONGEST STREET IN BROOKLYN IS BEDFORD AVENUE AT 8 MILES.

daydreaming. In the later years I channeled those daydreams into material for fiction, but in Decatur Street I still hadn't reached that stage of practicality, and my daydreams were just invented and thrown away.

As to what those daydreams were, I can scarcely remember. Some were megalomaniac in nature. I think I used to imagine, in great detail, waking up someday to find that I could play the piano beautifully, and surprising everyone with my ability; or being a master swordsman à la d' Artagnan; or in other ways demonstrating an unexpected and impressive virtuosity.

Oddly enough, I'm quite certain I never imagined myself to

imagined would be unsafe, and probably none of them was. Nowadays, of course, only a person intent on suicide would harbor Fred's ambition. . . .

One eccentricity I had that no one knew about, because I was careful not to talk about it, was my love of cemeteries.

In exploring the Decatur Street neighborhood, I found that three blocks southwest lay some cemeteries. The nearest was Trinity Cemetery, a small and crowded Catholic cemetery that didn't interest me. Another, though, was a large Protestant cemetery, the Cemetery of the Evergreens, just beyond Trinity. It was perhaps two-thirds the size of Prospect Park (Brooklyn's

off in the summer, I would take whatever I was reading at the time, preferably a science-fiction magazine, and go off to the cemeteries. In 1933, *Astounding Stories* had been taken over by Street & Smith Publications, Inc., and under the editorship of F. Orlin Tremaine it scaled new heights and became far and away my favorite science-fiction magazine.

Sometimes I would explore new avenues in the cemetery, and before long I had a whole series of favorite stone benches where I could sit under trees with no signs or sounds of human life or human artifacts in any direction.

In fact, the only thing that

A S I M O V

be a prolific writer. . . . My good friend and fellow writer, Fredrik Pohl, whom I was not to meet for some years yet, but who was growing up in Brooklyn contemporaneously with me, was more systematic about his walks. He got himself a street map of Brooklyn and began taking long walks. It was his ambition, he said, to walk through every single street in Brooklyn, and mark them off on the map as he walked through them till every one of them had felt his step.

I don't know that he ever completed this monumental task, for there are hundreds of miles of streets in Brooklyn, but the point was that he was not afraid to walk anywhere. There was not a street in the borough that he

largest) and was very much like a park that was unobtrusively interrupted here and there by gravestones.

I found that wandering about in it was delightful. It had the advantages of a park without the disadvantage of being full of people. I had been in parks; in fact, when we were younger, and before we had a candy store, a rare treat was that of taking a trolley to Highland Park and picnicking there. Highland Park was, actually, just on the other side of the Cemetery of the Evergreens, but I didn't bother trying to go there.

Cemeteries, of course, are full of the remains of dead people, but that didn't bother me. Whenever I could get a few hours

ever intruded into this lonely Eden (it was remarkably like being in a room with the blinds pulled down—just as cozy and separated from the world) was once when the caretaker stopped me as I went in—he knew me well by that time—and asked me, in a rather embarrassed tone of voice, not to whistle as I walked through the cemetery, because it offended the occasional mourners there. For a moment I was astonished that there would be mourners; what could they be mourning? Then I remembered, apologized and whistled no more.

That was another thing. I whistled constantly. Other people might chain-smoke or chew gum; I whistled.

I whistled popular songs of the day. I whistled Gilbert and Sullivan. I whistled Italian operatic selections. This undoubtedly bothered the people I passed, and that would occasionally be reported to my mother, and she complained about that. The whistling mania has decreased with age, but it never has vanished. In fact, I even sometimes absentmindedly sing in public. This is all usually interpreted by others as signifying that I am happy (and they sometimes say so in what seems a pettish annoyance, as though I have no right to be). And they are right. I am usually happy.

Fortunately, none of the complaints lodged against me did anything to repress my ego or individuality, because no matter how many times I was reported, and how many times my mother stormed at me for risking the family welfare by being eccentric, I nevertheless continued to do exactly as I had been doing. I had gathered the notion somewhere that my eccentricities belonged to me and to nobody else and that I had every right to keep them. And I lived long enough to see these eccentricities and others that I have not mentioned come to be described as "colorful" facets of my personality.

After P.S. 33, which was like an elemen-

tary school, I went to P.S. 122, and then to Eastern District High

School. I think the biggest thrill I ever had in my young days was

being picked for the Hall of Fame. This was something the

World-Telegram used to do. Lester Bromberg was the basketball

R E D   A U E

writer, and each week he'd pick certain high-school athletes for

what they called the Hall of Fame. You'd go down to the paper

and have your picture taken, and the next day everyone in the

city would see it. That was really something. Don't forget, I was

going to a high school that had mostly girls. We had about

R B A C H

General manager of the Boston Celtics basketball team

twenty-five hundred students and I'll bet at least eighteen-hundred of them were girls. We had no football program or anything like that, so most of our athletes in my area went to Boys High or Hamilton. Hell, we were just a little school on a concrete lot. There were no trees outside the door. There wasn't even a blade of grass. No one had ever been picked for that kind of honor from Eastern District before, so it was really kind of a special thing when it happened to me. Later, when I was a senior, I was picked All-Brooklyn, Second Team. Whenever I mention that to pro athletes they look at me and laugh. Naturally they've all made All-American teams and things like that, and they think All-Brooklyn, Second Team, was some kind of joke. Big deal! Well, it so happens it was a big deal. New York City was the mecca in basketball then. They tell me about Indiana and I say that's a lot of crap. New York is where all of your great players were at the time: your great LIU teams, the St. John's teams, the CCNY clubs, great, great NYU teams. Almost all of them were filled with New York City kids. So I'd remind my professional friends that making All-Brooklyn, Second Team, was a hell of a lot harder than making 80 percent of your All-State teams in the rest of the country. Whether people believe me or not, that was quite an accomplishment.

One day I was walking down the corridor at Eastern District High and the phys ed teacher—a man by the name of Alvin Bor-

ton—grabbed me and put me right up against the wall. "Let me tell you something," he said. "I happen to know you can be a pretty good student. Basketball's fine, but if you think it's going to carry you through the rest of your life you're wrong. It's nice to be a big shot, but there's no reason you can't earn good grades, too. So if you're thinking of college, you'd better get your mind on the books."

I respected this guy and I knew what he was saying was absolutely right, so I started to calm down a bit and pretty soon you could see my grades going up.

Then one day some kids came up to me and asked if I'd be interested in running for president of the student body. I was an athlete—captain of the basketball team—and no athlete had ever run for school president before. We lived in our own world and the real serious students—the ones who always became presidents—lived in theirs. But I liked the idea, so we started checking to see what the qualifications were. You had to have an 85 average. I was okay there because my marks were all around 87 or 88, a solid B. And you had to have a clean record. I had never gotten into any trouble, so I was all right there, too. I got some friends to join the ticket, and we started to campaign. We already had the sports crowd with us and most of the tough guys came over to our side. But the main student body was the big question. The guy I was running against had just missed winning the year before, so ev-

eryone regarded him as a shoo-in this time.

I had to stand up in front of the whole student body and make a campaign speech and, boy, I'll tell you, I was scared. I had never done anything like that before. So I started in: "Friends—friends in the true sense of the word—in fact, I might say I'm a personal friend of the greater majority of those present here today—you may wonder, perhaps, why I seek this coveted position..."

My goddamn knees were buckling, my stomach was all squeamish, and I was talking in a falsetto. While I was suffering through it, I made up my mind that if I ever got to college I was going to take a speech course. Other people could get up there. Why not me? But I was elected, the only guy in the school's history to be basketball captain and student president at once.

Then I discovered that the only damned duty I had was to get up and read the Bible at assembly time. I did it once and they never asked me to do it again.

Health columnist for

The New York Times

J A N E

My fascination with science and nature

can be traced to the insatiable curiosity of a little girl living in

the Manhattan Beach section of Brooklyn. The streets of Man-

hattan Beach have names arranged by the letters of the alphabet

and we lived on the first street, Amherst, one block away from

the ocean. As a child, my favorite pastime was exploring the

beach to collect the natural wonders that came from the water. I

would scavenge the rock jetties and find starfishes, clams, mus-

sels, snails, seaweed, and beautiful marine stones, then hurry

home to show off my treasures. Most times, because they smelled

BRODY

awful, my mother refused to let me in the house. She did let me play with all this stuff on a table and fish tank that was set up on the porch. I spent hours on end on that porch, playing with my little critters I found near the ocean. The joy I find in exercise and fitness was also inspired by the ocean. It played a big part in the family's recreation. My father was an avid swimmer who first taught me how to swim when I was three. Every morning from early May through late September, the whole family went to the beach and swam in the ocean. It was a daily ritual before school and work. He would swim laps between the jetties, in calm or choppy water. As I got older and stronger, I'd swim the jetties with him.

Although Manhattan Beach was a stable, middle-class neighborhood, my parents struggled economically, and subsequently were frugal with their expenditures. They taught me and my brother how to shop. My mother,

for instance, would never buy anything that wasn't on sale. Even if the more expensive dress looked better, she would select and settle for the dress that cost a little less. My father's specialty was produce. We would tour several fruit-and-vegetable stands in Brooklyn, where he would negotiate great bargains. He was especially adept at buying produce that the owner was just about ready to throw out. My father was a self-avowed expert on selecting fruit that was on the cutting edge of bad. After closing the deal, we'd race home and devour our purchases before they spoiled. When I went away to college, I finally allowed myself the luxury of buying fruits and vegetables that didn't have a stopwatch attached to them.

My father reminded me of a Norman Rockwell country doctor. He possessed the kindest, sweetest, gentlest soul, and was especially attracted to children. He loved to banter with the kids in the neighborhood or with children in passing cars. A man of boundless energy, he was the type of person who always needed to be doing something. He couldn't sit still. My mother would always implore him in her famous words, "Sidney, sit down already!" I inherited that restless trait. Though he was educated as a lawyer, he never practiced law. He held various jobs including a post in the state supreme court working as a clerk, and another time he opened an appliance store. Because of that appliance store we were one of the first families in Manhattan Beach to own a television set, a boxy cabinet with a seven-inch Motorola television screen. An odd feature of that television set was the huge magnifying glass that swung over the front. When the magnifying glass was placed in position, the tiny seven-inch screen expanded to an *incredible* twelve-inch screen. That was high technology in the fifties.

In direct contrast to my father's energetic style, my mother was a methodical woman with a wonderful sense of humor. She was a dedicated teacher who taught elementary school in the Gerritsen Bay neighborhood, and was many times rewarded by the wonderful letters she received from her former pupils. She was especially proud of one student, a shy boy with a fine singing voice. His name was Julius LaRosa, a student she particularly cared for in school. When he became a popular singing star on the successful *Arthur Godfrey Show*, she was delighted

for his success. My mother would sit in front of the television set and be extremely proud of his achievement.

Sunday was family and going-out-to-dinner day, and my favorite Sunday dinner was deli, especially those big, fat hot dogs called "specials" you'd get at a kosher deli. We'd drive to the deli and buy some "specials," tongue, pastrami, corn beef, rye bread, pick a big sour pickle out of the barrel, add some sauerkraut, and wash it all down with a Dr. Brown's Cel-Ray soda. It was a great Sunday feast. We would alternate our visits to the kosher deli by traveling the following Sunday to the Chinese restaurant with an all-Cantonese menu.

Achievement was a word that played a prominent part in our household. I grew up in a family where school and the importance of education was valued. There was never a sense of sexism. I was allowed to pursue my dreams and aspirations. At the age of four, I announced my intention to be a veterinarian. My father's response was that Cornell University was a school with a good veterinary science program, and if I worked hard I could fulfill my ambition. He never ridiculed my visions, never limited my horizons. My parents supported my dreams as much as my brother's. When I developed an interest in the piano but my family couldn't afford to buy one, a cardboard keyboard was fashioned for me to practice on. I practiced on the cardboard keyboard and the school piano,

DURING THE 1920s UNIFORMED FEMALE TAXI DRIVERS CRUISED BROOKLYN STREETS IN SEARCH OF A FARE.

until several years later when we were able to afford a spinet.

Encouraged by both parents to excel, school became a prime factor in my life. In addition to attending the regular school curriculum. I participated in all kinds of extracurricular activities. I joined the boosters at James Madison High School (I was a little chunky to become a cheerleader at the time), and became involved with the Madison Sing. With a classmate, I edited the school newspaper. One edition that was especially popular was a lampoon issue that parodied the school's principal and some of the school's silly rules. And though I wasn't an active member in the student government, many of the meetings were held in my apartment.

One of the most emotionally wrenching experiences during that time was enduring my mother's sickness. She was ill my entire senior year in high school. College was a year away, schoolwork was mounting, and I was participating in the extracurricular activities. Nevertheless, I wanted to visit her every day at the hospital in Manhattan, so I found time to do my homework on the subway rides to and from the hospital. One week before graduation, my mother died. Though I had graduated first in my class, I was determined to stay at home and be close to my father and brother. My grandmother argued that I must go to Cornell. She vowed that if it meant her going back to work to support my studies, I should still go away to college. I finally

agreed. The wonderful support I received from my family during that time has never been forgotten.

To promote the fun and gaiety that could be found at the Brooklyn shore, this crew of "lifeguards" was formed. They became so popular, Life Magazine featured them with a cover story.

JOSEPH

Secretary of Health, Education and Welfare under Presidents Lyndon Johnson and Jimmy Carter

We lived at 1030 Park Place between

Brooklyn and Kingston avenues, opposite the Children's Museum, on the border of Crown Heights and Bedford-Stuyvesant.

The neighborhood was mainly comprised of Italians and Jews,

along with a number of Irish and black families. My mother was

a schoolteacher, a graduate of Columbia Teachers' College. In

those days if you were a bright woman when you got out of high

school, you could apply to Columbia for training in their one-

year education program. That abbreviated program proved to

be a good training ground for many teachers who eventually

CALIFANO

taught in the New York City school system.

While my mother dedicated herself to teaching, my father was forging a career at IBM, then a fledgling company taking up all of three floors in an office building. He started his career as an office secretary, and, through long hours and hard work, worked himself up to the position of office manager for IBM's world trade division. Both of my parents identified very strongly with their work and, since I was their only child, I was expected to seriously apply myself in school, and during the summer, finding work was a foregone conclusion.

When I was fourteen, I got my first job at *The New Yorker* as a messenger. Every year after, summer meant another part-time job in and around Brooklyn and Manhattan. Those stints included a job at the neighborhood grocery, working in a florist, being a runner for the Wall Street firm of Brown Brothers Harriman, in the days before computer transfers when stock sales were pigeonholed, and working in the Paper Handlers Union. I particularly enjoyed working for the Paper Handlers Union. I'd help transport the huge rolls of newsprint that were stored on the docks or in warehouses to the newspaper plants around New York. While each of these jobs had its own merits, the most exciting job was ushering Brooklyn Dodger games at Ebbets Field. I was given this grand opportunity because of my good schoolwork at Brooklyn Prep High School. Brooklyn Prep was

an excellent high school that offered a fine Jesuit education. The teachers were very strict, yet very sensitive to what motivated their male students. One incentive they offered was attractive part-time job opportunities based on our performance in the classroom. The most appealing job was, of course, ushering a Brooklyn Dodger game. During my junior and senior years, I was rewarded several times with the opportunity to usher Brooklyn Dodger games. It was a great thrill working Ebbets Field on a crisp spring afternoon, enjoying the excitement of a Dodger game, and making pocket change, too.

While I was working in the LBJ White House, a chance meeting I had in Brooklyn was the impetus for a program I created under the Small Business Administration. I was invited back to Brooklyn Prep in 1966 to speak at their first-ever alumni dinner. Traveling with me from Washington was another Brooklynite, Jim Reynolds, then Undersecretary of Labor. Reynolds, it turned out, grew up only a few blocks up from me. He was looking forward to the Prep dinner, and was scheduled to make some opening remarks before introducing me. Before the function began, we decided to rent a car and tour the old neighborhood. One of the places I wanted to visit was the local candy store on Kingston Avenue and Sterling Place. The store was run by two affable Jewish fellows, who, by now, were quite old. When I entered the store and introduced myself, they immediately recognized me as a kid from the old neighborhood, but the nostalgia was dimmed by the sadness of their dilemma. The neighborhood had dramatically diminished and the store was doing very bad. Their resulting economic situation and their ad-

vancing age were forcing them to sell their store. They preferred to sell to a minority family in the neighborhood, but unfortunately hadn't found an eligible buyer. As they described their predicament, they became more forlorn. Their situation was an example of the hardship many small business owners were experiencing around the country. When I returned to Washington I outlined and implemented a program under the Small Business Administration that would help small business owners sell their stores to minority buyers. The buyers would also be assisted by the SBA. It was a win-win program for both sides and proved very successful. I was proud the idea for such a program evolved from a visit to my old neighborhood in Brooklyn.

J A C K

Popular television and

nightclub comedian

FOLLOWING PAGES:
BROOKLYN WAS ALWAYS
KNOWN AS A MAGICAL
PLACE. DURING THE TURN OF
THE CENTURY, THE ELEGANT
SPIRES OF CONEY ISLAND'S
LUNA PARK CAPTURED THE
IMAGINATION. IN THE 30S,
MANHATTAN BEACH WAS
THE HAVEN FOR MOVIE
STARS AND SOCIALITES.
TAKING A BREAK FROM THE
STAGE, SOPHIE TUCKER
RELAXES WITH HENRY
YOUNGMAN AND PAULA
KELLY. THE FELLOW IN THE
MIDDLE IS JOHN PHILIP
SOUSA III.

Growing up in Brighton Beach during the

late twenties and early thirties was like living in fairyland. I was

born in Harbor Hospital in Coney Island and lived in an apart-

ment in the back of my family's candy store at 219 Brighton

Beach Avenue, two blocks away from the boardwalk. Coney Is-

land was then an international attraction and nicknamed the

"Playground of the Kings." I was struck by the distance some

people traveled to come to Coney Island. From April through

September it felt like the neighborhood was throwing a party.

Directly across the street from the store was the elevated

C A R T E R

Brighton Beach subway line. I would stand outside and marvel at the thousands of beachcombers and amusement-park revelers who came streaming down the metal subway stairs. When a newly arrived train screeched to a stop, another horde would spill out, all dressed in their brightest summer outfits. The flow of people never ceased, and I could sense their bubbling enthusiasm and hear their excited voices on the subway platform overhead.

Because we were so close to the beach, we had seasonal customers who rented beach lockers my father set up in the cellar or in the backyard. Next door to the candy store was a popular restaurant that catered to the well-heeled Coney Island crowd. It was a special thrill to see the famous stars and vaudevillians who were performing at the Brighton Beach Theater. People like Al Jolson, Georgie Jessel, Sophie Tucker, Eddie Cantor, and all the performers from the Zeigfield shows would come into the candy store after a dinner at the restaurant. My interest in show business was sparked by

meeting these larger-than-life stars.

Winter months were also fun. During the off-season when it was quiet on the beach, my friends and I would jump a fence and have the stilled magic of Coney Island all to ourselves. We'd run around the amusement park in between the rides and game stands and have a grand time playing. We'd top off the day be enjoying the Nickelodeons and for a nickel each we'd get a raisin cake, a glass of milk, and a short movie. Adding to the charm of the neighborhood were

the people who worked in Coney Island.

Off-season, many of them lived in the Brighton Beach area. So the odd assortment of Coney Island characters who came into the store included the carnys and circus freaks. The Dog-Faced Boy, the Fat Lady, and Pip and Pep, the girls with the pointy pinheads, were regular customers. It was always enchanting meeting and talking with these people. When I wasn't running around Coney Island or working in the store, I spent hours at the Tuxedo Theater, a movie house specializing in horror movies. The film that especially frightened me was *King Kong*. Because my bedroom window faced the elevated subway tracks across the street, I had nightmares that King Kong was going to climb the tracks, reach into the window, and snatch me from my room. This nightmare lasted for quite a few nights after seeing the movie.

The theatrical aura of Coney Island prompted me to perform. I was ten years old when I first worked in front of people. I liked to sing and do impersonations, and I started my career on a kiddie hour in Brooklyn called *Aunt Shirley's*. I won a big cake for singing a 1932 song called "Let's All Sing Like the Birdies Sing." My father was very proud of me for winning the contest and, in those days, when candy stores had tables and chairs, he'd lift me up on a table to sing or do impersonations of Jimmy Durante or Edward G. Robinson. I was always a big hit performing for the customers in the candy store.

Although there are wonderful recollections of my years at Brighton Beach, the heartbreaking memory of my father slaving in the candy store has tarnished some of those memories. Seven days a week, from early morning to very late at night, my father's life revolved around the candy store. He'd begin his workday at 5 A.M., heading off to the wholesale market to buy ice and milk and then return to set up the newspapers on the outside stand. At one in the morning, twenty hours later, he'd lock up. This grueling schedule demanded more than one pair of hands so most of the family's activities centered around the store. Alternating with my father and mother, my two older sisters and I took shifts running the store. Especially hectic, of course, was the summer season. We'd eat lunch and dinner in shifts. The only time I can ever remember all of us eating together was on Jewish holidays when the store was closed. Though I was still quite young, I could sense there wasn't too much fun in my parents' lives and, as a result of this brutal schedule, by the time he was thirty-five my father had become very old.

When I was a young teenager, we moved to yet another candy store on Eighteenth Avenue in Bensonhurst. For a long time I was lost without the excitement and glamour of Coney Island, but I soon became best friends with a kid named Mario Mello despite my mother's warning to stay away from Italian boys. She felt the Italian boys in

the neighborhood would be a bad influence on me, but Mario was a sweet, quiet guy, from a fine northern Italian family. Ironically I corrupted him. I convinced Mario to buy a zoot suit so we could fashionably strut around the neighborhood. We'd spend days fishing in the Atlantic Ocean on the forty-foot cruiser his family had built, and on weekend evenings we went to the neighborhood dances. The friendship was interrupted when the war broke out and we both went into the service. After arriving home from a furlough one day, I announced to my father I was going over to Mario's house. Without looking up, my father said, "Jack, don't go there." Fearing the worst, I assumed Mario had died in the war. I was shocked to learn that he had died in a car wreck. After flying home to be with his wife, who had just given birth, he died on the way to the hospital. He was a great friend and a wonderful guy who possessed the courage to fly countless missions for the Air Force. It was such a tragic way to die. That day was one of the worst days in my life.

SHIRLEY

Former congresswoman from
New York's Twelfth
Congressional district

Although I was born in Brooklyn, I spent a

good part of my early adolescence on a Caribbean island. When

I was two and a half, accompanied by my three sisters, an aunt,

and her three daughters, I boarded the cruise ship *Vespers* for a

ten-day journey to Barbados. We were sent by my parents so my

mother could return to work to supplement my father's income.

Their plan was to save enough money to buy a home and pay for

our college education. When we arrived in Barbados, we were

met by my maternal grandmother, a stately woman who stood

six-feet-three-inches tall. A Caribe Indian who lived on a farm,

CHISHOLM

she was a woman who stressed discipline, religion, and education. Our duties included milking the cows, gathering the chickens in before a storm, and devoutly attending Sunday services. When I returned to Brooklyn eight years later, I found it very difficult to adjust to the urban mores of New York City's streets. The claustrophobia of the city, the high energy of its people, and the open discrimination against people of my color were in stark contrast to my previous experiences. In short, I had contracted a bad case of culture shock.

From the beautiful expanse of a rural farm, I moved to the Brownsville/East New York section of Brooklyn, into an apartment at 110 Liberty Avenue. My father and mother, Charles and Ruby St. Hill, were still struggling, he as a laborer in a burlap-bag factory in Brooklyn, she as a seamstress and domestic. During my first year back, my mother would send me to run errands around the neighborhood. I would get lost on almost every occasion because I wasn't comfortable following street signs. In Barbados, directions were followed by a series of landmarks, and I brought this thinking with me to get around. While running my mother's errands, I'd select vantage points that usually were stores or residential buildings. Unfortunately, as happened on more than one occasion, the stores I had chosen just a week or two earlier, either went out of business or changed façades. It was all very confusing

and precipitated recurring incidents of a police car stopping in front of my house to return me home. The sight of a police car, with me sitting in the rear seat, caused many of our neighbors to wag their tongues. They all wondered aloud how a child raised in such a strict and disciplined environment could have turned out so bad.

Besides adjusting to the confusion of the Brooklyn streets, school became a problem for me, too. During my last year in Barbados, I completed the sixth grade in a British elementary school, but when I enrolled into P.S. 84 I was immediately demoted to the third grade. The principal explained the demotion due to my lack of knowledge of American history and civics. Growing bored with the easy subjects of the third grade level, I became an avid spitball thrower, mischievously hitting the other kids when the teacher wasn't looking. My parents were summoned to the principal's office, and after a series of such meetings, it was decided that I should be skipped ahead to my proper grade and given a tutor for my American studies. At once I immersed myself in my schoolwork and settled down.

Unfortunately several other adjustments I had to deal with weren't that easy to change. The kids all laughed at and made fun of my West Indian accent. The hazing went on for some time. Because I was a spunky child, I defended my honor by beating them up. After word got around the school that I was a tough kid who didn't take any nonsense,

the teasing stopped. The other problem was more serious. The first time I was called a nigger by a male classmate, it went completely over my head. In Barbados I never heard the word, but when my friends told me its implications, I got very angry. The next day I returned to school and gave him a good beating, which earned me yet another trip to the principal's office. Although I didn't realize it at the time, I was learning to live and cope in America through my fists. It wasn't that I was innately bad. In truth, I was very excited about the new environment and trying desperately to fit in. But I had yet to grasp the limitations that were being placed upon me in this new setting, the attitudes, beliefs, and prejudices that I hadn't experienced in Barbados.

During the summers I would sell newspapers to make pocket change. I worked a better job later on helping the old Jewish women at the Brownsville Markets on Sutter Avenue and Belmont Avenue. Because of the proper way I spoke, and my ability to handle the English language above and beyond that of my peers, I was in great demand to help these woman explain their wares to potential customers. Their goods ranged from vegetables to fabrics. I would go from cart to cart explaining their merchandise to interested buyers. At the end of the day, I skipped happily home, proudly holding dear my precious fifty cents for the day's labor. I would visit the local candy store and buy bags of candy, incurring a reprimand from my mother, a disciplinarian as strict as my grandmother.

It took the better part of four years for me to completely assimilate into the American life-style. By this time I was enrolled in Girls High School and living on Ralph Avenue in the Kingsborough Housing Project. The more I learned about the plight of the black person in America, the sadder I became. Part of my despair was seeing how other people lived. I would walk with my girlfriends along Eastern Parkway, which was a lovely neighborhood at the time, and gaze at the grand houses and apartments. We'd peek into those beautiful homes and hope that we'd have a chance to live that way. I decided then that one day I would get a job to help my people.

I was eighteen when I won my first amateur ballroom dancing contest at the Savoy Ballroom in Harlem. I was known in my Brooklyn neighborhood as a terrific dancer, a girl who was a bundle of energy on the dance floor. My specialty was the lindy hop, and everybody in the neighborhood knew that if Shirley St. Hill was coming to a party, there'd be lots of fun and dancing. Though I wasn't doing anything wrong—I was participating in the culture of the times, just like all the other kids—my enthusiasm for dancing and singing was frowned upon by my mother. She would say to me that she thanked the Lord I had a good brain, otherwise I would sink further into a world of sin. My father, a more liberal

parent, tried to convince her to ease up a bit, but she was intransigent. A classic episode was the night a young man escorted me home after a party. I was about twenty at the time. My mother would sit near the apartment window when she expected me home from a party. She knew how long it should take for me to get from the street to the apart-

ment's door. Well, I guess I took a little more time than she thought was necessary. Just as the young man leaned over to give me a good-night kiss, the apartment door flew open, my mother grabbed me by the ear and pulled me in. The young man stood there, in the quiet solitude of our hallway, completely flabbergasted.

THE PUSHCART MARKET IN BROWNSVILLE, WHERE FRUITS, VEGETABLES, FISH AND MANY OTHER STAPLES WERE SOLD, WAS A SHOPPER'S PARADISE.

BARRY

Down the street from my two-family row

house on Van Siclen Avenue in East New York was the Jamaica

Bay swamplands. It was an ominous place that me and my

friends, as grade-school children were forbidden to explore. Al-

though I played with an adventurous group, we nevertheless

stayed away from the area, confining our activities to the other

end of the street. One day, however, I made my first trip into

those swamplands. As I approached walking side by side with my

father, I could see the plane that moments before had dropped

from the sky. It was a small, private plane, and the eerie sight of

Celebrated scientist and
environmentalist, director of the
Natural Biological Sciences
Department, Queens College,
New York

COMMONER

it lying upside down in the marshes was simultaneously frightening and fascinating. As frightful a sight was seeing the pilot, dangling in his harness, hanging from the plane's cockpit. My fears about the swamp gradually disappeared as my father and I hurriedly trudged across the spongy turf, with other neighbors from Van Siclen Avenue, to save the pilot from the wreckage.

Van Siclen Avenue was in many ways a bucolic setting in the early 1920s. Across the street from our house was a goat farm that ran from one end of Van Siclen Avenue down to the other end. The sight of cart plows, powered by teams of horses used to dig up the earth, was common, too. My elementary school, a few blocks away, had unheated toilets in a separate building. It was a grueling adventure to run out to the bathrooms in the middle of winter. One of the first intrusions of urban progress was the construction of the elevated subway nearby. Because rivets were used to join steel girders together, sitting underneath the skeletal elevated structure was a huge furnace attended to by a laborer. As he slowly opened the door to pull out a glowing red rivet, the flames of the furnace would light up the street. In a very smooth motion, the furnace man would then throw the hot rivet to another laborer sitting on a girder overhead. The rivet would be caught in a metal funnel and then securely fastened into place. Although the process was laborious, the construction of the elevated structure moved

along quite rapidly.

My parents were Jewish immigrants from Russia with very little education. My mother, in fact, never went to school, although she did learn to read Yiddish and read practically every Yiddish novel. When she was twelve, she was already working as a seamstress. My father worked as a tailor and he had very little schooling himself. The person who inspired my intellectual development was my uncle, Abrahm Yarmolinsky, a younger sibling of my mother who had earned a Ph.D. in Europe. When he arrived in New York, he rapidly advanced and soon was administering the Slavonic Division of the New York Public Library system. I first asked for his help when I was given a grade-school assignment to write a paper on cotton. He took me to the nearby library in Brooklyn, showed me all the catalogues, and taught me how to look for the appropriate books and papers. On subsequent assignments, he continued to offer his expertise on the art of research and, upon seeing my growing interest in science, one day bought me my first microscope.

At James Madison High School, (we moved from East New York to 1082 East 32nd Street, between K and J, during my junior-high-school years), I was known as a science whiz kid. I first became interested in science in J.H.S. 149, where I built an electromagnet and then made a wireless Morse code clicker. My interest in nature was sparked by excursions to Prospect Park

DURING THE 30S AND 40S, TREE HOUSES WERE POPULAR AMONG KIDS, ESPECIALLY IN THE "SUBURBAN" PARTS OF EASTERN AND SOUTHERN BROOKLYN.

ABOVE RIGHT: TRAVELING LIBRARIES, DESIGNED TO ENCOURAGE READING HABITS AMONG CHILDREN, WERE AN EXTENSION OF THE NEW YORK PUBLIC LIBRARY SYSTEM THAT REACHED INTO ALL FIVE BOROUGHS.

and the Brooklyn Botanic Garden. I learned quite a bit at the Brooklyn Botanic Garden by working in the Children's Garden, growing vegetables, and becoming involved with all kinds of projects. I broadened my science interests by setting up a workshop in the basement of our house, where I conducted science experiments. I also became fascinated with electricity, which resulted in many blown house fuses. I developed an interest for inventing things, too, transforming a regular microscope, by adapting a very bright light using a carbon arc, to project on a screen what was in the microscope. The judges at a high-school science fair awarded me a prize for that invention. Because my experiments became more complex, which required tools I couldn't afford, I would improvise along the way. One creation was heating an ice pick and using it as a drill or finding old batteries and using them as sources of power. I remember how happy I was when I received my first pair of pliers, because that is one tool that you simply can't improvise.

My science aptitude paved the way for an after-school job with a lab supply company that eventually led to my first entrepreneurial pursuit. A local textile company came to me and asked if I could raise clothes moths. They had developed a mothproof chemical for wool, and they were planning an exhibit to show how the clothes moth larvae would eat ordinary wool, but not the treated wool. For a long time I struggled to raise clothes moths in my house, confining this particular experiment to my closet. Achieving little result, I continued my research and found that whale meat was the best way to raise clothes moths. After finally locating a store on the Lower East Side of Manhattan that sold whale meat, my clothes-moths experiment was finally successful. It was probably the very first time (and possibly the last) that clothes moths were raised in a Flatbush apartment.

A A R O N

Composer

For a long time I harbored the pleasant

notion that I was a child of the twentieth century, having been

born on November 14, 1900. But some authorities claim that the

twentieth century began on January 1, 1901. I calculate there-

fore that I spent my first forty-eight days in the nineteenth cen-

tury—an alarming thought! Unlike some creative artists, I have

no memory of a lonely childhood. It seems to me I was always

surrounded by people. Certainly, at birth I must have been

stared at in my crib by my four considerably older siblings:

Ralph, twelve, Leon, ten, Laurine, eight, and Josephine, seven. I

C O P L A N D

might have been stared at more by my father and mother if they hadn't been so preoccupied with the management of the source of our livelihood: a fair-sized department store located at the corner of Washington Avenue and Dean Street in Brooklyn....

The daily routine at the store was demanding. Saturdays and Sale Days were particularly exhausting, and Christmas was the busiest time of all. I distinctly remember "helping out" in the toy department (after school, of course)...I occasionally acted as relief cashier when the regular employee was off duty. The cashier's perch was a balcony area near the ceiling from which one could survey most of the premises. Cash and sales checks arrived with a bang via a system of wired "trolley cars," which gave the post a certain dramatic punch. But most important was the responsibility and trust the job implied. Artists have usually been thought to be nitwits in the handling of money. No one has ever accused me of that particular failing....

On Sundays we generally visited relations in Manhattan or the Bronx, where Grandma Mittenthal lived with her youngest son, Nathan, who never married. I particularly recall a visit to our affluent branch, the Uris family, at their roomy apartment on upper Madison Avenue. When spring came, the family went on outings down Ocean Avenue to Brighton Beach in our horse and buggy (the same horse that pulled the delivery wagon on weekdays). By 1914 or thereabouts, we bought our first automobile. One felt like an ab-

BUILT AS A MONUMENT TO THE UNION ARMY IN 1892, THE SOLDIERS AND SAILORS' MEMORIAL ARCH STANDS ABOVE GRAND ARMY PLAZA NEAR THE ENTRANCE OF PROSPECT PARK.

FOLLOWING PAGES: THE BEAUTIFUL AND CLASSIC DESIGN OF THE BROOKLYN MUSEUM HAS INSPIRED VISITORS SINCE IT FIRST OPENED ITS DOORS TO THE PUBLIC IN 1897. ITS INVENTORY CONTAINS OVER TWO MILLION OBJECTS.

solute plutocrat riding around the neighborhood in that new gray Chalmers. Now on Sundays or holidays we were able to travel as far away as Arverne or Rockaway Beach. My older brothers Ralph and Leon drove, of course, but it was when my lively sister Laurine took the wheel that all heads turned to stare at the sight of a girl driving a car. I learned to drive the Chalmers from Laurine when I was about sixteen....

To my surprise, the idea of a composer of so-called serious music being born on a drab street seems to have caught the fancy of many a commentator. But that was the way Washington Avenue seemed to me in retrospect, long after I had left it. To any boy living there it would have seemed like an ordinary Brooklyn street. There were our neighbors, Vollmuth the baker, Peper the painter, Levy the butcher, the candy-store man across from our house, the large grocery store down the block (no chain stores yet), and of course, the corner saloon with its occasional neighborhood drunks. *Culture* could hardly be said to be a familiar word on our street, yet it wasn't entirely absent from the area. A ten-minute walk up Washington Avenue brings you to Eastern Parkway, where you will find the Brooklyn Museum. (It was there, aged ten, that I suffered my first "cultural" shock at the sight of a nude statue.) Ten minutes in the opposite direction from our house was the Brooklyn Academy of Music, where I heard my first symphony concert when I was sixteen....

Sometime before I was born, my parents had enrolled as members of Brooklyn's oldest synagogue, Baith Israel Anshei—Emes [situated at Kane Street and Tompkins Place] in downtown Brooklyn. (Founded in 1855, Baith Israel Anshei-Emes was known as Brooklyn's "Mother Synagogue.") On high holy days you weren't supposed to ride, and it took us about forty-five minutes to walk there. By the time I was almost thirteen and being readied with Hebrew lessons for my bar mitzvah, my father had been president of the synagogue for several years.... The part of my bar mitzvah I recall most vividly was the banquet—it actually took place in the store! Relations came from near and far. The merchandise was moved away and an area cleared where we could set up tables....

School life had begun in the usual way at age six when I was taken by my mother to be registered at Public School No. 111 at Vanderbilt Avenue and Sterling Place. Our school was situated in the midst of a "nice" neighborhood—that is to say, Sterling Place boasted rows of upper-middle-class houses with brownstone fronts. But the trouble was I had to pass through a few blocks near St. Patrick's Catholic School on Dean Street, and that was always "dangerous territory." A Jewish boy had to watch for himself. For whatever reason, I recall the tough trips to school, but I seem to have blotted out the eight years of grammar-school attendance—teachers, fellow pupils, and all. I

did my homework, moved ahead each term in the usual way, and graduated from P.S. 9 in 1914....

Mr. Leopold Wolfsohn was giving piano lessons to the Uris children. His claim to distinction in our minds was that he was a teacher from Manhattan who spent one day a week in Brooklyn, giving lessons in a rented studio in the old Pouch mansion at 345 Clinton Avenue. It took some convincing for my parents to agree to my piano studies—after all, they had paid for their other kids without remarkable results. But they finally agreed. It was typical that no one in the family accompanied me when I went to arrange for lessons with Mr. Wolfsohn. My parents always had a kind of basic confidence in me—"If he thinks he can do it, let him do it." Fortunately for me, Wolfsohn was a competent instructor, with a well-organized teaching method....

From the fall of 1917 to the spring of 1921, were years that represented much more to me than the study of piano, harmony, counterpoint, and form. What made them truly stimulating was the sense I had of uncovering a whole cultural world outside the field of music that I gradually became aware of in my growing-up years. This sense of discovery was doubly exhilarating because, for the most part, I found it out myself. It was at the Brooklyn Public Library on Montague Street that I made my acquaintance with Sigmund Freud, Havelock Ellis, Romain Rolland's *Jean Christophe*, and Walt Whitman's

"I Hear America Singing." Reading became a passion second only to music. Along with this came a broadening of my musical horizons. I can still recall the thrill of coming upon racks of music scores in the dingy upstairs corner room at the library. And what was equally surprising was the fact that music scores, like the books downstairs, could be borrowed for study at home. I learned to orchestrate by borrowing scores from the library. When I knew I was going to hear something performed, I imagined what it would sound like, took the score to the concert, and followed it to see whether it matched what I thought I was going to hear. The difficulty was that they used to turn down the lights very often, so that you couldn't see. I remember an embarrassing incident when I was looking forward enormously to hearing *Pelléas et Mélisande* for the first time, and I think it was the Chicago Opera Company that came to the Brooklyn Academy of Music with a one-shot guest performance of this "odd" work. I got myself all prepared in my seat up in the gallery with a little searchlight and the score—the piano-vocal score actually—because the other one would have been way out of my price range—and I waited till all the lights went out and then quietly turned my light on. Well, I hadn't gotten beyond two pages when an usher dashed up and said, "Turn that light out, you dope! Turn that light out!" and my whole plan collapsed. That must have been around 1918.

ABC-Radio Network sportcaster

During my years at P.S. 9, we lived on

Lincoln Place, between Underhill and Washington Avenues. It

was a narrow street, as I remembered it, and it was even nar-

rower than I remembered it when I went back to look at it.

Number 329 was where we lived. It seemed a nice, happy place

then. We used to go down to the cellar, open the window slightly,

fronting on Lincoln Place, take out our pea shooters, and plague

passersby with the sting of our carefully aimed missiles. Then

we would scurry away with exultant chuckles at the discomfort of

our targets. We would build snow huts every winter in back of

HOWARD
COSELL

49

Dixon Harwin's house next door. His family had money (his father was a doctor) and they had a private home right next to our apartment building. As if to prove their wealth, they even had a pool table in a downstairs playroom. Dixon went on to the University of Pennsylvania and all the guys on the block envied him. He was one of the older guys on the block, my brother Hilton's age.

Hilton is four years older than I. Lincoln Place was a wonderful world of sports, dominated by Hilton's age group. There were guys like Jack Storm and Al Thorner, pure stylists when it came to punchball. Al was a master at looking at first while he punched the ball over third. Jack was one of a kind. He could do everything, a white Willie Mays of the street.

I was lucky if I could even get into a game because I was so much younger. That's why I remember a day when I was the last one picked just to fill out a team. They put me in short left field, close to the third baseman, and Jack Storm hit a screaming liner right at me. In self-defense, I put up my hands and the ball stuck in them. I was an instant hero. The next inning I made two errors and got kicked out of the game....

I got my introduction to music in those years—if you call it music. Every Sunday morning, my dad would get out his fiddle and play. He loved light opera; Victor Herbert and Rudolf Friml were his pets. It got so that I would hum "My Hero" from *The Chocolate Soldier* for an entire

week. He alternated between that and "The Donkey Serenade" for an hour or more, screeching away, until my mother would finally say, "Izzie, that's enough. You're driving us crazy." Then he would smile sheepishly, put the violin in its case, and take Hilton and me rowing on the Prospect Park lake. After that we would have a milkshake. Those were the days. Some Sundays we would have to visit my paternal grandparents. My brother and I rebelled at all these visits because we wanted to be out playing, but we were quashed. The one redeeming feature was when we went to Brownsville to see my dad's folks. There was a candy store nearby that made the best milkshakes I have ever tasted, creamy and rich....

My dad was not a good-looking man, but he had great dignity in his bearing and in his face. He looked a lot like Henry Morgenthau, Franklin Roosevelt's secretary of the treasury, with the same rimless, pinched-nosed glasses, the same smile. Dad had one habit that drove us all mad. Every Sunday morning, before he would start to play the fiddle, he would take every shirt he had out of his bureau drawer, carefully examine them, refold them, and put them away. Don't ask me why.

The real arguments in the house would occur over other things though, things like his preoccupation with his family; the fact that as controller for a chain of clothing stores, he was almost always on the road; the further fact that his job was nei-

ther high paying nor secure....When I would hear and see my parents quarrel I would cringe. I made a vow, then and there, that when I married, my children would never witness an argument between my wife and me. That has turned out to be the case almost, not quite, but almost.

I fell in love for the first time in my life on Lincoln Place. Her name was Dorothy Schroeder. She was a beautiful Scandinavian, blond, about eleven years old, and lived on the same floor we did in the apartment building next door. It happened in a thoroughly orthodox way. One night I was in our kitchen and she was in hers. The shades were not drawn. I looked through our window at her, and she looked back at me. I smiled, and so did she. And then, heavens know why, we started matching kitchen utensils through the windows. I would hold up a pot, so would she. Then a knife. Then a fork. It went on for fifteen minutes, until there was nothing left in the way of objects. I finally mustered up all my courage, blew her a kiss, and she blew one back at me. After that, every night for the next two weeks I would go to the kitchen, look over to see if Dorothy was there, and hope for a reprise. It never happened. My love went unrequited, and I never had the nerve to talk to her when I would see her in the street.

Actor

As I lay in my bedroom on Hawthorne

Street, I always knew when my Dodgers were doing well. Ebbets Field was six blocks away, and the excitable roar of the evening's crowd would thunder through my window. Based on the enthusiasm of the cheer, I would surmise that one of my heroes had just blasted a pitch over an outfield wall, or a fireballing Dodger pitcher had struck out an enemy batter. Those guessing games were a delightful evening ritual, a wonderful prelude to falling asleep. Although I was ordered to bed early as a youngster, and denied permission to follow the game on radio, I could share the

JON
CYPHER

crowd's excitement in my bedroom. There was nothing better than waiting for the roars from Ebbets Field to begin. That grand old ballpark was a wonderful anchor for the lively world of Flatbush, a neighborhood filled with great vitality.

My parents separated when I was an infant, and as a result I never knew my father. My mother moved in with her parents, into a brownstone building at 21 Hawthorne Street. She worked for thirty years as a fourth-grade schoolteacher at P.S. 204 in Sheepshead Bay, so it was expected that I, the son of a teacher, would do well in school. Education and scholastic achievement were important to my friends, too. Their parents instilled in them the value of doing well in school and of someday attending college and achieving a professional status. The belief that one could move up, socially and economically, through a good education, pervaded the neighborhood. With the encouragement and support I received from my mother and grandparents, and motivated by the competition with my friends, I worked very hard to attain good grades in school.

My grandparents were immigrant Lithuanian Jews who assimilated easily into Flatbush life. A favorite food treat they especially enjoyed was the freshly baked, seeded rye bread and the schmalz herring at Louie's Delicatessen, a popular store across Flatbush Avenue. Every other day when Louie baked new loaves of seeded rye bread, my grandmother would give me a dime

ANCHORING THE FLATBUSH COMMUNITY—IF NOT ALL OF BROOKLYN AS WELL—WAS EBBETS FIELD, HOME OF THE BROOKLYN DODGERS.

and a penny and send me off to Louie's. Because of its popularity, the place was always bedlam. The store bustled with activity, jammed to the doorway with hyperactive, old Jewish women, elbowing their way to the counter to make their purchases. To avoid getting swallowed in the crowd, I'd crawl my way through the commotion, sneak up to the counter, buy the rye bread and herring, and scoot out the door.

Singing is a very important part of my life, in fact, it was my first step toward my acting career. I made my stage debut as a ten-year-old singing "Bless This House," in front of a P.S. 92 assembly. My early singing was nurtured by a frail, elderly gentleman who rented a small room

in my grandparents' brownstone. He was a retired violin and voice teacher, who was drawn to me from the time I was a little child. On many occasions he'd give me a voice lesson and teach me old folk songs. I grew close to this very gentle man who heartily encouraged me to sing, and I was deeply saddened the day an ambulance came to take him away. I was losing my friend. The day he left, he leaned over to me and whispered that one day I would be a fine singer. Six years later, at the age of fifteen, as I lay in a hospital bed listening to an aria from *Martha*, I was struck by the melodious beauty of Enrico Caruso's voice. I was moved so deeply I decided my life's ambition was to become an opera singer. To fulfill that goal, I practiced and worked on my singing during my years at Erasmus Hall High School, joining the chorus, becoming president of the chorale group and eventually singing with the All-City Chorus under the inspiring direction of Peter J. Wilhousky. I eventually placed second in a singing audition for the Juilliard School of Music, singing the same aria from *Martha*. Several years later, while finishing my college years at Brooklyn College, I decided to expand my horizons by enrolling in acting school.

A vital part of Flatbush was the diversity of the street vendors and sidewalk singers who passed through the neighborhood. Vegetables, fish, strawberries, flowers, ice, and milk were just a few of the items sold by these vendors. Larry the Ice Man would deliver a block of ice, hoisted by huge steel tongs, into a family's apartment for twenty-five cents. In the summer he'd chop off several slivers of ice with his pick and give them to the kids to suck on. The clippety-clop of the horses that pulled the Sheffield Farms milk cart resounded through the street during the morning. Most of the people on Hawthorne Street kept an insulated milk box in the vestibule of their homes, and many a morning I was awakened by the clanking of the milk bottles. During the early evenings, little bands of German street singers would serenade the neighborhood. Made up of three or four singers, their tunes were accompanied with vi-

olins, clarinets, and trombones. In appreciation, the neighbors would throw pennies from their windows. The neighborhood was like a little carnival, a world unto itself. Flatbush, home to the largest Jewish population in the world at the time, was a polyglot community with large numbers of Germans, Swedes, Russians, Latvians, and Ukrainians. Because of the number of languages spoken in the neighborhood, I unwittingly developed a keen ear for identifying the various accents.

During the war, when the Brooklyn Navy Yard was at its peak, sailors rented rooms in the two rooming houses across the street from our brownstone. Their presence in Flatbush hastily expanded my juvenile horizons. During our many af-

ternoon excursions into Prospect Park, which we imagined to be our own Sherwood Forest, my friends and I often found condoms under the bushes in the more remote sections of the park. These vestiges of passion titillated our adolescent fantasies, as we lustily imagined the scenario the night before. Occasionally, during the late evening, when the street was quiet and everyone was asleep, some of the sailors would sneak their lovers up to their rooms. If I was awakened by their noise on the street, I would get up from my bed and excitedly peek out my window, peering across to the newly lighted window, hoping a shade would be left drawn open. Of course, much to my disappointment, I was always denied.

BEFORE THERE WERE HOUSEHOLD FRIDGES AND FREEZERS, ICE MEN STOPPED IN FRONT OF YOUR HOUSE TO CHOP OFF A BLOCK OF ICE.

V I C

When I hear old recordings of Glenn Mil-

ler, Benny Goodman, or Tommy Dorsey, I immediately relive

the moments and wonderful memories of my days in Brooklyn.

Brooklyn will always be a very special place for me, the setting

where I learned about life, friendship, family, and religion. I had

some close pals in Bensonhurst; in fact many of those friends

still live in the old neighborhood, and whenever I'm back East,

we get together and remember those great days. It may sound

hokey, but I feel I'm a very lucky fellow because of my roots in

Brooklyn, and I'll always cherish the special experiences I had

Singer

FOLLOWING PAGE: CHICKEN
FARMS, LIKE THIS ONE ON
SHEFFIELD AVENUE IN THE
NEW LOTS SECTION OF
BROOKLYN, WERE A COMMON
SIGHT IN BROOKLYN DURING
THE 30S.

D A M O N E

there.

The parish of St. Finbar's, the neighborhood church near my home at 288 Bay 14th Street, played a particularly important role in my life. For many years I sang in the church choir as well as at the confraternity center. Father Donegan was a very special priest in the parish, a man who possessed a great amount of understanding and sensitivity for his parishioners. While I was in elementary school I became an altar boy, and I would often serve Mass with him. During the service it was inevitable that I would goof up, but Father Donegan never got angry or chastised me on the altar in front of the parishioners. Rather, he would offer a quiet smile or pat me on the head, or whisper encouragement to keep trying. To show my appreciation for his sensitivity, I'd make sure he'd get extra wine in his chalice when he celebrated the offertory part of the Mass.

Choir singing at St. Finbar's was the result of my mother's persistence. She was a piano teacher and a strict disciplinarian who would grab me by the ear and force me to practice. We would vocalize together and run the scale at least thirty to forty-five minutes a day. Most times I would sing during these sessions with one eye and ear on the activities taking place in the street. My only interest at the time was playing ball. I wanted

to be with the guys! Summer days were the most agonizing. I would be vocalizing with my mother and have my catcher's mitt in hand. As I practiced, I would beat the mitt with a ball, but she paid little attention to my impatience. She was determined that I make something of myself and because she felt I had some talent, she was adamant in nurturing it along.

Although I was investing a great deal of time in singing, I never thought of it as a professional career. One day, however, I heard something on the radio that finally inspired me, the catalyst that ultimately provided the spark. It was a Sunday afternoon and I was sitting in the apartment on Bay 14th Street, huddled over a big plate of pasta.

As I ate, I was listening to *The Brad Phillips Show*, which that day was featuring a Battle of the Baritones. Frank Sinatra's rendition of "A Ghost of a Chance" started to play. I was a growing young teenager and it took a lot in those days for me to walk away from a hot plate of pasta, but I was genuinely spellbound by Sinatra's voice. I moved near the radio and because my four sisters were making their usual racket in the apartment, I edged closer to the music by pressing my ear against the speaker. If I'd gotten any closer, I would have been inside the cabinet. Sinatra's interpretative style of the lyrics was absolutely mesmerizing. What he was doing with the words and the sounds he was making with his voice at that mo-

ment was remarkably enchanting. I closed my eyes and began singing with him, slowly recognizing, as I sang, that I could make the same sounds he was making and achieve almost his same tones. I was amazed that I could emulate his style and realized at that moment just how much I loved singing. I decided then to earnestly pursue it as a career.

At sixteen I dropped out of Lafayette High School to support my family because my father had been in an accident. Previous to my leaving school, I had worked as a part-time usher at the Deluxe Theater in Brooklyn and from there moved to the Loews Oriental on 86th Street. When I quit school, I found another usher job at the Paramount in New York. While working at the Paramount I was taking singing lessons for a dollar a week, which in those days was quite expensive. Although my mother thought I could sing and I felt I had some talent, I didn't know what anybody else thought. During one of Perry Como's engagements at the Paramount, I finally got some feedback. In addition to being an usher, I doubled as the elevator operator. One evening, as I took Como up to his dressing room on the fifth floor, I politely asked him if I could sing him a few bars. I decided that if he thought I had potential, I would continue with my singing ambitions. If I got a negative reaction, I'd move on to something else. As we made our way up, I sprang the question and he said "Go ahead, kid, sing." I stopped the elevator between floors, turned to him, sang four bars, and stopped. I figured that was enough because I didn't want to waste his time. He told me to keep singing. I sang another four bars and stopped again. This time he told me to finish the song. After I finished, he complimented me on my voice and asked me to sing for his bandleader after his show that night. Como then wrote a note to Johnny Long, a bandleader who was playing at the New Yorker Hotel. Long was looking for a vocalist and Perry thought I could fill the bill. Although Long had already hired a vocalist by the time I got over to the New Yorker, Perry Como's generous encouragement and support that day gave me the confidence I needed to keep going.

I finally sang my way onto the stage of the Paramount, opening my act during the Christmas season with the Stan Kenton Orchestra. Eight months later, at the age of eighteen, I had my first hit record. Although I was a popular singer I still considered myself one of the guys in Bensonhurst. Many of my Brooklyn friends would hang out backstage while I sang in front of the audience. With the money I earned as a singer, I bought my family a home on 86th Street and 12th Avenue, and continued to live in Brooklyn while I had my radio show. When I signed a contract with MGM Pictures in 1950, which required a move to California, I reluctantly said good-bye.

CLIVE DAVIS

I came from a family that encouraged two

types of education: what I learned in the streets was equally

important as the knowledge I absorbed in school. The streets of

Crown Heights during the late thirties and early forties were

swarming with children, so groups of playmates were generally

delineated by age. Just a year difference in age meant you

played in another group. There were so many kids, the nine-

year-olds played with their peers, the ten-year-olds with theirs,

and so on. My street experiences consisted of hanging out on the

front stoop of our Union Street apartment and participating in

the games of the day. I loved playing sports and played every game imaginable, including stickball, hit the penny, and Chinese handball. Because I was one of the better athletes in the neighborhood, I was usually one of the first kids to be selected when teams were chosen. After a full day of playing in the street, we'd sit on the stoop in the evenings to wait for the Night Owl edition of the *New York Daily News*. As soon as it was delivered to the corner candy store, we'd grab a paper and check the progress of our beloved Dodgers. The next day we'd repeat the same ritual. Besides sports, music was a big interest in the neighborhood. The boys and girls would constantly argue about the most popular singer. Most of the girls liked Frank Sinatra, while the boys preferred Bing Crosby and Perry Como. My favorites were Kay Starr and Dinah Shore. Occasionally we'd all take in a movie at the Savoy or Albee, but

the big event was taking the train into the city for a stage show at the Roxy, Radio City, or the Paramount.

The commitment to excel in street games was also applied to my schoolwork. I was extremely involved at P.S. 161, a terrific school staffed by interesting and motivated teachers. In a lot of ways, my childhood identity revolved around school. Most of my friends were from my class and my straight A average put me in good stead with the teachers and principal. When I graduated from P.S. 161, I was subsequently awarded the Boys' Scholarship Award for highest average. Upon entering Erasmus Hall High School, I again found a learning environment that was conducive to a great education. Everyone at Erasmus was genuinely enthusiastic about the learning process: The teachers were stimulating and exciting, the administration fostered a collegelike atmosphere, and the student body viewed education as a way to

FOLLOWING PAGE: ORIGINALLY AN INDIAN PATH, FULTON STREET IS THE OLDEST STREET IN BROOKLYN AND THROUGH THE YEARS ONE OF THE MAIN SHOPPING VENUES IN DOWNTOWN BROOKLYN.

move out and up from their lower-middle-class station in life. P.S. 161 prepared me to do well at Erasmus Hall, which I did by continuing to carry a straight A average.

Family, of course, played a big part in my life. Our ground-floor apartment at 1321 Union Street was lovingly tended to by my mother while my father was busy selling electrical supplies. Because my mother's family lived in the Crown Heights area, we saw may of her relatives on a daily basis. Weekends, however, were reserved for my father's side, when we'd travel to Coney Island to visit Zaideh and Bub-

beh. My father's parents were immigrants from Russia and respect for the older generation was very important. At an early age I was taught the custom to first kiss and acknowledge my grandparents before greeting anyone else.

Without a doubt the most important force in my life was the well-rounded education I took with me from Brooklyn. The camaraderie I developed with the other children in the street endorsed the value of getting along with others. The built-in competitive structure in the melting-pot environment manifested itself on the street and in

the classroom, which eventually carried over into the business world. The fine education I received from P.S. 161 and Erasmus Hall High School equipped me with the skills necessary to move ahead. Almost every teacher I had in P.S. 161 I remember vividly today, more so than my teachers in New York University or Harvard Law School. It was an education that was enormously beneficial. I look back on Brooklyn as an invaluable experience not only with extreme pride, but with great nostalgia and affection.

JERRY

I was born on the north side of West 7th

Street in Gravesend and then moved to the south side of the

street when I was a child. In the grand scheme of the neighbor-

hood, West 7th Street was "good," which meant that although we

might have (and we did) an occasional criminal (or an occasional

DELLA

"He's away for a while" situation), we didn't have out-and-out

shooting in the streets. When we reached junior high school we

began to break the rules. But I could begin to see the difference

even then: some of us were breaking the rules and some of us

were breaking the law. A group of us who were not into active

FEMINA

lawbreaking had stumbled across a truck that was partially hidden in one of the innumerable dumps around the neighborhood. No one was going to find that truck deliberately unless they knew exactly where it was. The truckload of radio tubes originally had been hijacked by a gang of guys who lived on West 10th, West 11th, West 12th, and West 13th streets and Avenue U. *They* were regarded as the crazy ones in the neighborhood, hotheaded enough to go with guns and masks and force the driver of a truck to turn over thousands of dollars' worth of radio tubes to them....

At the age of fifteen, we were a bit frightened of what we were doing when we took the tubes. It was a two-way thing: we knew that what we were up to was strictly illegal; and we knew that if the guys who had done the original stealing ever caught up with us, we would be in very deep trouble. They would not be hampered at all by any moral restraints; if they had to kill us to make a point, they would.

Four blocks away from fairly straight West 7th, things were much worse. West 10th was a very tough street and the four-block difference in criminal intent had more to do with geographic origin than it did with family income. We all were poor, but West 7th Street was more Neapolitan and West 10th was strictly Sicilian. The immigrants from Sicily brought with them closer contact and knowledge of the Mafia, while people leaving Naples simply did not have the exposure (or the in-

volvement). It was this elementary geography more than anything else that colored the neighborhood's attitude toward law and order....

The toughest kids hung around one particular candy store called the Rat Hole. It's still there, although it has been boarded up for years. If we had a potential cop killer growing up on West 7th Street, he wouldn't hang around our candy store—you'd find him lounging at the Rat Hole. When the kids in the neighborhood realized that the crew on West 10th was truly dangerous, we went out of our way to avoid them. My candy store was on MacDonald Avenue and I stayed there for years, never venturing into the Rat Hole....

All of the "connected" guys drove Cadillacs. They didn't wear pinky rings, but they dressed better than anyone else. When a connected guy was expected in the neighborhood of Avenue U—there would be a sudden awareness *he* was coming. No one would know precisely how this information was received, except that it was always accurate. Soon a flashy car would ride up, and a soldier of the local family would emerge. He'd be dressed simply—white shirt, pair of dark slacks, jacket—and usually he would conduct his business with someone very quietly near the candy store. That seemed to be very important, somehow, because in all of these comings and goings I never saw any of the wise guys go *into* the candy store. They always talked *near* the store. At a safe distance, the neighborhood

watched with avid curiosity. All of the gamblers, the bust-out guys, the hangers-on, the potential hoods, the kids desperately wanting to become connected were trying to stay cool and unconcerned, but they were watching. After all, this was our version of royalty.

The only thing of value I took with me into the real world after living *through* my neighborhood was the ability to spot instantly in a crowd who really holds the power. I learned this watching how the true Mafia guys would conduct themselves and how we would identify them. It is the same as going into a corporation boardroom and wondering who the leader of the company is. Whom do you have to win over today? Today, if I meet with five or six men, I can spot the individual who *pretends* to have the power, and I also can immediately perceive who truly *is* the strength behind the pretender. It is exactly how things were when I grew up. You knew almost at once who were the blowhards, the storytellers, the braggarts, and who had the clout. The true Mafia guys had a way about them; they walked differently, they carried themselves with a certain confidence that the ordinary punks in the neighborhood just didn't have....

Forgetting the Mafia, plain law and order was a rather difficult concept for Avenue U. Ask any resident of the neighborhood today what "law and order" is and it's a probable eight to five he won't know. In the next breath mention that some interesting goods have just arrived at a neighbor's house and if this fellow is interested in a size 42 brown cashmere overcoat for sixty-five dollars, no questions asked or state sales tax to bother with, watch his response.

It was quite possible that suddenly, in an obscure neighborhood of Brooklyn, a hundred and fifty men would turn up wearing the same brown cashmere overcoat, size 42, in fact the same lot number from one of the manufacturers who supplied Brooks Brothers with brown cashmere overcoats. We didn't find this cloudburst unusual, and we won't in the future. The coats simply fell off the truck.

On one famous occasion—absolutely true, I swear to God—I could have walked into three hundred homes in my neighborhood, gone into three hundred bathrooms, looked at the three hundred toilets, and suddenly discovered three hundred identical toilet-seat covers (plastic jobs, dainty pink), which happened to be that week's "special."...

Although only a handful of people were suppliers, all of us bought. The world cannot resist a bargain, and we were no exception....

The point to remember is that buying hot goods was so ingrained that no one thought it wrong, immoral, or against the law. There were few outside mores reaching our neighborhood. Consequently, the neighborhood did not know that rest of the world thought trafficking in hot goods was illegal.

The news of a shipment spread quickly. I can remember guys coming around the house flashing a suit saying, "Look. We're going to come in and show you all of the suits at once. Get your family and friends in at the same time." It was a sort of Avon Lady party of our day. While my friend was making arrangements for people to come in for a suit, we weren't sitting around making moral judgments that this is buying stolen goods and it's wrong. Rather it was, How are we going to get Cousin Ralph (who weighed maybe 250 pounds) into a size 40 suit?...Incidentally, there were no checks, no credit cards, no charge accounts. Cash on the line. The "salesmen" never had any credit problems.

My family shopped regularly...and never thought about it. One spring a truckload of iridescent green jackets hit the streets and I got one. It took me until the age of sixteen, when I got to the outside world, to realize that the whole business was wrong. Today, my mother has (reluctantly) quit this type of shopping...because she's afraid of what I might say. She'll show me something she's bought and my first question is, "Is it hot?" Her answer is, "Don't be silly, you know we don't do that kind of thing anymore."

WHEN EUROPEAN IMMIGRANTS BEGAN SETTLING IN BROOKLYN, THEY BROUGHT WITH THEM MANY CUSTOMS FROM THE OLD COUNTRY. FOR ITALIAN IMMIGRANTS, A GAME OF BOCCE BROUGHT BACK MEMORIES OF THEIR NATIVE LAND.

D A N

Financial columnist and

TV commentator

ELEGANT ARCHITECTURE
HAS ALWAYS BEEN PART OF
THE BROOKLYN LANDSCAPE,
ALTHOUGH MANY BUILDINGS
FELL TO THE WRECKER'S
BALL. THE OFFICES OF THE
LONG ISLAND WAREHOUSE
AND STORAGE COMPANY
WAS AN EXQUISITE BUILDING
LOCATED ON NOSTRAND
AVENUE.

OVERLEAF: THE
GOTHIC DESIGN OF THE
RAYMOND STREET JAIL,
BETWEEN WILLOUGHBY AND
DE KALB STREETS.

I spent a good portion of my life in the

smoky din of Maxie's poolroom in Williamsburg. Maxie's was my

home. Not my home away from home, mind you, but *my home*! I

learned how to survive by understanding what you can and can't

do with a cue ball. I made money when I was a kid hustling pool

and Ping-Pong at Maxie's. I would never play up to my true

ability, just enough to beat the other hustlers out of their money.

I played a little poker too, anything that could get me through

the day. Getting by usually meant another hard salami sandwich

to eat and a few extra dollars spending money. My parents di-

D O R F M A N

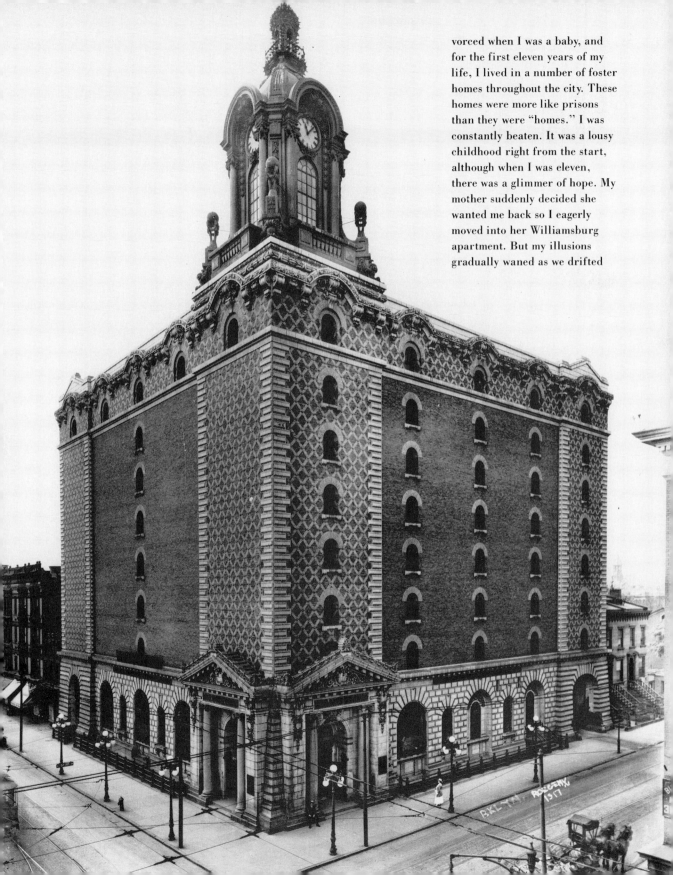

vorced when I was a baby, and for the first eleven years of my life, I lived in a number of foster homes throughout the city. These homes were more like prisons than they were "homes." I was constantly beaten. It was a lousy childhood right from the start, although when I was eleven, there was a glimmer of hope. My mother suddenly decided she wanted me back so I eagerly moved into her Williamsburg apartment. But my illusions gradually waned as we drifted further apart. She made it clear she wanted her life to herself. My father, Max, was a garment worker and every time I saw him he was drunk. He literally drank himself to death. The situation at school wasn't better either because I was basically a loner. I didn't get along with any of the kids, and there wasn't a teacher who inspired me in any way. The only faith and trust I had was in myself and my ability to hustle money at Maxie's.

Besides hustling pool and Ping-Pong, I ran errands for some of the guys in Murder Inc. I remember meeting a couple of those guys, and I particularly recall an incident one day when one of them called me over to the stoop he was sitting on. He told me to run across the street and buy him a sandwich. The sandwich shop was *literally* across the street. When I returned with his lunch he gave me a three-dollar tip. I couldn't believe it. All that money for going across the street. That was quite a lot of money in those days, especially for a kid. I thought I was rich. I remember looking at him, all dressed up, and thinking to myself that whatever he was into I wanted to do. If I had gotten into his business, I would have ended up killing people for a living.

High school was a disaster, particularly the years I went to the New York School of Printing, a vocational school in Manhattan. That school, like the foster homes I had been bounced around in, was the same: a prison. The kids would beat up on each other, and they had this particular fascination of taking

their anger out on me in the elevators of the school. While in high school, I continued to survive by hustling money. I was delivering telegrams for Western Union when I worked out a deal with the owner of a Brooklyn cafeteria. This place was a joint that attracted the neighborhood bookies. I set up a concession in the bathroom, and after the guys finished their business, I'd hand them a paper towel and whisk broom the back of their coat. One guy who was a regular was nicknamed Rats. His scam was a pegboard business. You'd pay to stick a pin through the hole of a small pegboard. The unraveled piece of paper that was pushed through would reveal your winnings. He'd go around the neighborhood with his board selling pinholes to all the neighbors and businessman in the

area. He earned his dubious title because he would kill rats and glue their hair around his shoes as decoration. Besides the bookies and con artists, there also were the guys who made a living by beating and maiming people. That was the element who drifted into that place. I survived by being shrewd, clever, and keeping my mouth shut.

What my times in Brooklyn taught me was to be cynical and skeptical of anyone who crossed my path. Not to allow myself to trust too many people. My parents, the foster homes, the neighborhood characters, high school, and hustling pool all prepared me well for learning how to survive. That meant keeping my head screwed on straight in Brooklyn, or thriving in the business world.

V I N C E

The fire hydrant on Pleasant Place in East

New York gushed the sweetest tasting water I've ever drunk. To

escape from the heat of a blistering summer day, I'd curl under

the cool spray of the fire hydrant and take in a mouthful of water.

It always tasted great. I relished the taste and feel of the water,

jumping into the invigorating spray to escape a sweltering day's

heat or dragging a milk crate underneath for an early evening

bath. As was the case on other Brooklyn streets, we played street

games under the surge of the fire hydrant and, with our hair

matted down from the soaking, chased the neighborhood girls

Actor

FOLLOWING PAGE: SUMMER
RELIEF! THE SPRAY OF A
FIRE HYDRANT WAS THE
BEST WAY TO COOL OFF IN
THE STREETS.

E D W A R D S

around the street and pulled them under, too. They would squeal and scream in mock horror, but they enjoyed the cool relief just the same.

Although I knew many of the kids who hung around Pleasant Place, Fulton Street, and Rockaway Avenue, I was a boy who basically went off on my own. My enjoyment was staying in the house and doing some of my own things, like building model airplanes or reading. I was the youngest of seven children, as well as being a twin, but in many ways was raised an only child. When my brother Anthony and I came along in 1928, there was a nine-year difference between our older brothers and sisters. I can still hear the clamor of activity in the house on 11 Pleasant Place, my family sandwiched on the second floor in between my grandparents on the ground floor and my aunt upstairs. It seemed everyone in the house was always going off somewhere, leaving my mother and me at home.

Because I spent a lot of time with her, my mother developed a deep interest in my future success. Our extra closeness developed, I suppose, because I saw more of my mother than my twin. He was the extrovert who would always be out in the street playing with the guys. Because of our close relationship, my mother pushed me a lot harder to do better during my school years at P.S. 155 and P.S. 73. There were many afternoons—on those days when I was playing out in the street—when she would come out on the stoop and order me in to do my homework. Although she was especially strict with me, her support was always positive and optimistic.

When I was twelve years old, my parents separated and, because my older brothers and sisters were at an age to begin their own lives, my mother, Anthony, and I moved into a three-story house on Marion Street in Bushwick. We lived on the top floor over Dr. Rosenthal, who maintained an office on the second floor of the house. My mother got a job as his receptionist. Around this time swimming started to become a big part of my life, and because my ambition was to go to Yale, I decided I would swim my way to a scholarship. The same energy and effort I put into my schoolwork I dedicated to swimming, and by the time I was thirteen I was winning club championships.

During my early teens, many afternoons and evenings were spent in a swimming pool, perfecting my technique and improving my time. The Flatbush Boys Club was my home away from home, and because it kept me off the streets and was a way to get to college, my mother approved. By fourteen, with my strokes perfected and faking my age, I took a job as a Coney Island lifeguard. This was a

dream come true. Not only would I be able to work on my swimming during the summers, I would get paid for it, too.

Lifeguarding at Coney Island was everything I expected it to be. It was a job that mixed lots of fun with a tremendous amount of responsibility. Weekdays on the beach were the best days of all, because the water wasn't crowded with bathers. By Sundays, the crowds swelled to what seemed like a million swimmers and I'd spend the weekends pulling people in danger of drowning out of the water. For many years I worked the Bay 14th beach, next to the Steeplechase pier, right in front of the Parachute Jump. Along with two other lifeguards, I worked a full day's shift, rotating from the stand on the beach to the catamaran on the water. I especially enjoyed being out on the boat near the breakers, where I could enjoy a nice summer breeze.

The people who came to Bay 14th always took care of the lifeguards. They would bring us lunch, a sausage sandwich, bacon and egg on a roll, or a hot-pepper hero. It was a wonderfully festive atmosphere except for those times when someone drowned. With the number of people who came to the beach, there was always that possibility. And because of the tremendous crush of the people in the water, it was hard for a lifeguard to monitor everyone's safety. The very first time I saw a floater, I went into a state of shock, but after a couple of years, though, I got used to such sights.

A big bonus for the life-

guards was working "dawn patrol." Although you were required to be at the beach at six in the morning, I made it my business to be there earlier. Dawn patrol consisted of "sweeping" the beach with a large rake, essentially cleaning the sand for the day. On any given morning, you'd sweep up lots of things. Weekends were the best days because the bounty of riches found was directly proportional to the number of people that used the beach the day before. On really good days, I would sweep up a couple of hundred dollars in change, paper money, and jewelry. So despite seeing the occasional drowning, Coney Island lifeguarding was a great job with lots of side benefits. Meeting and talking with the people on the beach, working dawn patrol, and getting my swimming practice in to earn a scholarship to Ohio State University were all worth the effort.

FOLLOWING PAGES: WHEN THE FIRE HYDRANTS COULDN'T CUT THE MUSTARD, THE WORLD HEADED FOR THE SHORES AND AMUSEMENTS OF CONEY ISLAND.

BILL

Publisher of Mad Magazine

On Sunday mornings my mother would send me off to Bible school, hoping to spiritually enlighten me. With the Good Book in hand, and the quarter she gave me for the collection plate burning in my pants pocket, I would sneak to the nearest candy store and buy the *New York Daily News*. Because we didn't get the *News* delivered at home, these digressions were necessary for me to continue one of my favorite passions: reading the comics. Although the church got cheated out of my weekly donation, it was at the expense of my following the exploits of Dick Tracy, Andy Gump, Gasoline Alley, and Little

GAINES

Orphan Annie. It was twenty-five cents well spent. I always loved the comics and still do. During my early years in Brooklyn, I also looked forward to reading *The American* to see what Maggie and Jiggs, Popeye, Happy Hooligan, and Slim Jim were all up to. Of course, much of my passion came from my father, who happened to own a comic-book business.

After several post-Depression years in the Bronx, my family moved to Brooklyn's Flatbush section, settling in at 1827 East 24th Street, between R and S. By the time we moved to Brooklyn, Maxwell Gaines, a former advertising agency executive, had gotten his *Famous Funnies* comic-book business off the ground and begun to flourish. In fact, Pop was one of the pioneers in the comic-book business. While working at an advertising agency, he thought of the idea of publishing comic books as premiums for consumer companies. This led to the notion of selling comic books on newsstands, and from there his business began. He was the fellow who discovered Superman, which he recommended to Action Comics, a competitor that needed a lead feature in its new magazine. So much for foresight! When my father died suddenly in a boating accident, I got involved in the business, and added a horror, suspense, science-fiction, and humor slant. We had nine comic books going when I started a tenth comic book in 1952. We called it *Mad*. While the other nine are long since gone, *Mad* continues and does

quite nicely.

Although the funnies and comic books were a big part of my life, they certainly didn't take up all my time. I spent a lot of time messing around the neighborhood doing activities which in retrospect held no intrinsic value, but were nevertheless fun things to do.

I especially enjoyed practical jokes. There was one exploit that got me and my friend, Billy White, into deep trouble with our parents. We decided one lazy summer afternoon to tie our sisters to a fence. We fashioned the ties using a water hose, and we warned them that if they struggled to get free, the hose would turn on and they would get soaked. There was no way in a million years we expected this to work, but by God it did! We paid for our little escapade when we got home.

Then there was the periscope episode. After learning how to make a periscope out of cheese boxes in science class, a friend and I got the crazy idea of constructing a six-foot model and hauling it down to Manhattan Beach to spy into the women's lockers. After carrying the monstrosity all the way down to the beach, we carefully leaned and positioned it against the locker-room wall. While my friend acted as lookout, I excitedly peeped into the periscope waiting for my boyhood fantasy world to appear. To my surprise and disappointment, I quickly learned women walk around locker rooms with towels on. We put a lot of effort into that one, and it got us nowhere.

When not playing practical jokes or dreaming up a foolish, mischievous scheme, I spent a lot of time at the Quentin movie house. The Quentin was the best bargain in Brooklyn, better than the Avalon and Kingsway. For a dime I watched three features, a couple of shorts, and a newsreel. My favorite movies were *Frankenstein*, *King Kong*, and *The Mummy*. *The Mummy* was particularly enlightening because that movie got me interested in Egyptology. After seeing *The Mummy*, I spent every Saturday for a couple of years at the Metropolitan Museum of Art, studying hieroglyphics. This knowledge came in handy during my college days at Brooklyn Polytechnic Institute. I scored an A for a paper on hieroglyphics, from a Brooklyn Poly teacher who was relieved to read something other than a scientific treatise.

I've always hated the sun, so I was never a beach-loving person, yet somewhat foolishly I persuaded my mother to rent a locker at Orient Beach. They were offering a kids' special, selling a season pass for ten dollars. Like a lot of other kids, I had an attitude: once something was attained, it was quickly forgotten. As soon as I got the locker, my interest in the beach waned. But at my mother's daily insistence that I go to the beach and not waste the ten dollars she invested, off to the beach I went. So with another quarter in my pocket to cover carfare and three hot dogs, I would ride down to the boardwalk, sit on a bench, and read a book. After the appropriate time, I'd head back home. There were days, though, I did enjoy my boardwalk excursions. Those were the afternoons

when the beach staged free concerts on the bandstand. They presented the most incredible entertainment. Victor Lopez and Betty Hutton, Tommy Dorsey, Benny Goodman, and Jimmy Durante all played on that bandstand.

One subject I had absolutely no interest in was sports. Yet, because I was the high-school monitor in charge of distributing the *New York Herald Tribune* in my high school, I was given the job of high-school sports liaison. I was assigned to cover all the sports activities that happened at James Madison High School, and report back to the paper. It became an Abbot and Costello routine. The poor reporter at the *Tribune* would telephone and question me on the coverage of a just-finished sporting event. Most of my coverage was summarily answered with "I don't know"s. It was obvious I wasn't giving him too much to use. I was lucky if I got the score right. One of the more memorable incidents in my sports reporting career was the day I covered my first football game. I was sitting on the bench with my hat on, furiously scribbling pregame notes. The band struck up "The Star-Spangled Banner." I was so involved and keyed up, I didn't hear it playing. I didn't stand up, and, worse, I kept my hat on. I took a lot of heat from school officials for that blunder.

My penchant for practical jokes and pranks continued through my late teenage years. When I was nineteen, I was made a sector warden for the air raid drills in the neighborhood, in

charge of a bunch of messengers. One benefit of the title turned out to be the water pump the Civil Defense issued to all their wardens. The water pump squirted an arc of water twenty feet away. On moonless Friday or Saturday evenings, we'd head down to Sheepshead Bay and hide behind a tree. At just the right moment, we'd squirt a smooching couple parked in their car. If we were really feeling our oats, we'd ride in a passing car and squirt all the kissing couples in one pass. Lest anyone think otherwise, we didn't limit ourselves to romantics. We'd spray commuters riding on trolley cars or unsuspecting people walking down the street. We'd have great fun with that water pump, using it in ways the Civil Defense didn't quite have in mind.

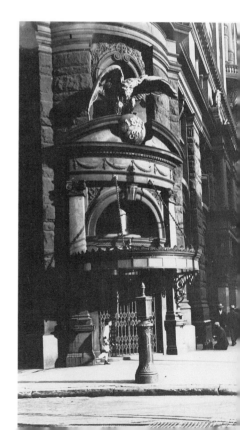

RICHARD

The idea of giving birth outside the home

raised a stir in the family. My grandparents were concerned

about my mother's desire to deliver in a hospital, because their

southern Italian values embraced the notion that "living and

dying" were done in the home. There was no need to include

strangers in such personal affairs, they argued, even if this was

America. Notwithstanding my grandparents' apprehension, I

was born an alert, healthy baby in a nearby Brooklyn hospital.

The south Brooklyn neighborhood of Red Hook was essentially

an Italian village imported to the "new" country. Adjoining the

FOLLOWING PAGES: MANY
IMMIGRANTS SETTLING IN
BROOKLYN FELT SICKNESS
AND DYING SHOULD BE
ADMINISTERED TO IN THE
HOME. THEY SHUNNED
FORMAL TREATMENT IN
PLACES LIKE THE BROOKLYN
HOSPITAL.

GAMBINO

Educator and author

entrance to the Brooklyn-Battery Tunnel, it was a self-contained Italian community that featured all the customs, attitudes, and beliefs of the newly arrived immigrant. Other than the occasional visit to Coney Island, the Brooklyn Museum, or Prospect Park, there was absolutely no reason to go outside the area. Anything that was needed to survive could be found within a few short blocks. Like most families in Red Hook, we lived as an extended family in a four-story brownstone. Quite charming in its time, it still had vestiges of elegance, featuring hand-carved woodwork, high ceilings, and large crystal chandeliers. The two bottom floors were occupied by my family and the two top apartments were rented by other Italian families. In the event our families needed to converse, my grandfather added an additional detail to the building by opening a space between his ceiling and our floor. The top apartment, where the Spano family lived, offered a panoramic view of the Statue of Liberty standing gloriously at the mouth of New York's harbor.

The integration of the Italian culture was incongruous to American conventions of the time. My grammar school, P.S. 142, was a classic example of this cultural dissonance. The ethnic makeup of the teachers at that school was mainly Irish and German, and they had little knowledge of Italian culture. Because of their ignorance, they harbored a deep contempt for the Italian student body. Unfor-

tunately, most of the teachers weren't shy about displaying their scorn. They berated us with remarks that questioned our intelligence, family values, or dignity. I particularly recall a teacher who, without provocation, violently slapped me in class, accompanied by an anti-Italian remark. And yet another teacher kept a basin of soapy water on her desk, and for the slightest transgression, she called a student up to her desk and washed his or her mouth out with soap. This woman was sadistic in the true sense of the word. We would go home and tell our parents about these goings-on in school but they would side with the teachers without investigation.

There was one teacher, however, who was very caring from those days, although it was I who let him down on a special occasion. Although there were some teachers who viewed me as a freak, the day they learned I scored the highest in the district on the citywide I.Q. exam, I was earnestly singled out by Mr. Fine to represent the district in a citywide proficiency examination in American history. After weeks of preparation, the morning of the exam I overslept. I had never overslept for anything in my life and looking back I guess I was struggling with my newfound success. Mr. Fine was very disappointed and angry with me, but to this day, I still nourish my love of American history by constant reading and research, an appetite inspired by Mr. Fine.

Being the firstborn son was royalty in the Italian household.

I was allowed to do most anything I wanted, so long as it was not illegal or something that caused embarrassment to the family. The street society was composed strictly of boys, while the daughters of the Italian families were not allowed to go out to play or hang out on the street. They were expected to stay inside and help their mothers with the chores of the house. The only experiences I remember with girls was the interaction with my female cousins when the families got together and with the girls at school. One particular schoolgirl with whom I was smitten in my early years in grammar school was a girl named Ramona, a very dark pretty girl, with large eyes. I was very embarrassed just being in her presence. I remember one St. Valentine's Day—a day that is celebrated here but meant nothing to Italian immigrants—when the mail came and amid the pile was an odd-looking envelope. I thought for sure the envelope contained a St. Valentine's Day card from Ramona but when my grandmother opened it and put it down on the table, all my hopes were dashed. It turned out to be a utility bill.

My father loved little children, and in many ways he looked at the world with a childlike innocence. Most Friday evenings he would announce to me that "tomorrow I am going to take you to see a surprise." One of his pleasures was exploring Brooklyn and Manhattan, and with me in tow we would enter the Carroll Street subway station and off we'd go on our Saturday morning journeys. Sometimes it

would be places in Brooklyn—Coney Island or Prospect Park—and sometimes it would be sights in New York City. He found America to be a fascinating place, a country with many possibilities, unlike Italy, where land, jobs, and money were hard to come by. He would marvel how you could do anything, be anything here in America, but at the same time he counseled me never to lose my heritage—not just my Italian heritage—but more important, to hold on to my Sicilian tradition and its values. This contradictory message to go out and make something of yourself, but at the same time "don't stray too far from your family's values," was very confusing. It was a message that was being echoed by many Italian immigrants to their American-born offspring and one that was the cause of much psychological confusion for first generation Italian-Americans.

My mother was a clear example of this confusion. She was part of a generation that was torn between the American values of moving up and out in the world, versus the conventions of the "old-world" Italian culture that subscribed to staying close to home. As a youngster, I sensed the troubled feelings that stirred in her because she was deprived of activities she wanted to pursue. I felt her anger and disappointment because she wasn't allowed to finish school. Part of the drive I have, the obsession for work, comes from my mother. Her words to me, "You can do what I wasn't allowed to do," became part of my psyche.

During World War II, my grandmother built prayer shrines inside her apartment to keep vigil for the safety of her sons fighting in the American army. These two shrines were fashioned with statues, candles, and pictures of saints. The candles burned day and night. I was impressed with the solemnity of these shrines, the somber glow of the candles, the soft faces on the saint cards, the frozen visages of the statues. She spent many hours near the shrines praying to St. Lucy and St. Rosalie, two revered saints in Italy. Even when she was away from the shrines, doing a chore in the house, for instance, she was always praying. Her prayers were a soft murmur and all in Italian. She kept track of the war by listening to the Italian radio station, WHOV-AM. Through the day, news from Italy was rebroadcast in Italian, offering updates on the progress of our armies. These somber news items were punctuated every so often by *Pasquale C.O.D.*, a comedy radio program that offered my grandmother comic relief.

Receiving a telegram when your son is off fighting in a war three thousand miles from home is a frightening experience for any parent. So it was as my grandmother stood in horror as she fumbled with the newly arrived envelope. Adding to her fear was the fact that she couldn't read what it said. In her terror, she hurried me upstairs for my mother, who would translate the telegram. My Uncle Joe had been wounded, it read, but the telegram didn't reveal the ex-

tent of his injuries. My grandmother began to cry, interspersed with murmurs of praying, hoping and pleading his injuries weren't severe. Thank God, as we were to find out a short time later, they were not.

One year later, after VJ Day, Red Hook celebrated the end of World War II with the biggest party the neighborhood ever saw. With colorful streamers hanging from rooftops, enlarged photos of my uncles and other neighborhood war veterans hanging in front of storefronts and houses, everyone came out to welcome the war vets. There was all kinds of food on makeshift tables and joyous music filled the air, and then finally my uncles arrived dressed in their army uniforms. My grandmother passionately hugged and kissed them, and was extremely happy that day, grateful, like many mothers were, her sons were finally home.

THE DIVERSITY OF FOOD FOUND IN BROOKLYN CAN BE TRACED TO THE VARIETY OF IMMIGRANTS THAT HAVE MOVED THERE. FROM PASTA AND BLINTZES TO KIELBASA AND HOMMUS, THE RANGE IS OVERWHELMING.

Actor

VINCENT

In the mid-1920s, when I was five years

old, I made my acting debut at the Fifth Avenue Theater in

Brooklyn. Located on 3rd Street and 5th Avenue, the theater

staged performances for the surrounding Italian community

with shows that were performed strictly in Italian. The part I

played that first evening was the lead role, portraying the life of

a small child who's left behind in Italy when his parents emigrate

to America. In the end, the child and the parents share a won-

derful reunion, but not before a great deal of melodrama. The

author of that play was my father, Gennaro Gardenia, the im-

GARDENIA

presario of an Italian theater company based in Brooklyn, and because of him the theater was to become my playground, my Coney Island, indeed *my life*, for the next sixty years.

During the 1920s, theater companies like my father's began to blossom all over Brooklyn. Because of the great influx of Italians to New York, Italian theater, in the various dialects, offered an inexpensive distraction from the hard life the immigrants found in their new country. There were other theater troupes acting in the Sicilian and Calabrese dialects, for instance, but my father's troupe was known as the best company that performed in the Neapolitan tongue. He was one of a handful of actors who worked the theater full time; most were part-time actors and singers who would work by day and perform in the evening.

After arriving here from Resina, a small town in Naples, in 1922, he quickly found success acting and singing his way through the theater companies that were already based in New York. In two years he saved enough money to have my mother and me travel here by boat. Because we had trouble finding an apartment (Italians were discriminated against during those years), my parents decided to rent a store on Sackett Street in a very rough neighborhood near the Brooklyn waterfront. The only way a family could live legally in a store was to sell merchandise out front. My father bought a small inventory of penny candy and placed it in the

window. We added a few cots and a stove in the back, and called it home. My mother, suddenly displaced from a small peaceful village in Italy, was scared to death of the rough characters who roamed the neighborhood. Whenever my father would go off to work, she would never open the door of the store. We didn't last there very long.

With the continued success of the Gennaro Gardenia Dramatic Company, we moved into our first home on 77th Street and 17th Avenue in the Bensonhurst section of Brooklyn. This home became our base for my father's business. When my brother and sister were born, my father took me under his wing because I was a bit too wild for my mother. So every day I would travel with my father to the theater, and I continued to be fascinated with all the costumes, makeup, lights, actors, and sets on the stage.

The company would perform six, sometimes seven nights a week. We'd play places like the Majestic Theatre on Fulton Street, the Casino Theatre, and the Star Theatre on J Street. Sunday was our biggest day, a chance to make quite a bit of money, and we'd pack the house at the Academy of Music. During the summer we'd play a lot of outdoor festivals or three-day block parties like those held on Court Street in Red Hook or in Williamsburg and East New York. One of my favorite places was the open-air theater on Bay 47th where we worked for a couple of years. The plays were always melodramatic and always

depicted the plight of the Italian immigrant.

As a child performing in an acting troupe, there was a great deal of tolerance for my lack of acting abilities. Any mistake I made on stage always brought a warm response from the audience. The fact my father was the leader of the company also helped. During the Depression years, there was one role I had that stopped the show. I'd sing a song of nostalgia that was sprinkled with some spicy innuendo. The audience absolutely loved it. After my rendition, I'd go into the audience and give away sheets of music to the song. They would tip me for the song sheet and there were many times I'd take home eight or nine dollars a night.

While performing in the evenings, I was enrolled in P.S. 186 in Bensonhurst. I was registered under my Gardenia stage name, instead of my real name of Scognamiglio, because the first day at school the principal had trouble spelling my name.

My father had been ill and my mother couldn't speak English, so one of the actors from the troupe was sent to register me. When the principal couldn't figure out the right spelling for Scognamiglio, the actor told him to use Gardenia. My father took me aside the day I was to enroll in Shallow Junior High School. He had been troubled I wasn't using my real name in school. He said acting was one thing but reality was another, so in the real world I should be known by the family name of Scognamiglio. We went down to the new school that day and had the name changed. Although I enjoyed school and the friends I made there, I couldn't wait until three o'clock when I would meet my father and head off to the theater. By the time I reached grammar school I was playing many of the juvenile roles he wrote for me. When I didn't have a role, I'd go backstage and try on the costumes, or explore the orchestra pit and the balcony while the play was on. Some nights I'd just sit in the audience.

My father was a very passionate man filled with much life and bravura. He loved to walk around with large hats and capes or coats draped over his shoulders. Quite often, after a performance, he would invite the acting troupe over for a midnight dinner. He loved having people in our home. The house on 77th Street became an enclave for many dinners and parties and I'd sit at the table with the other actors until I fell asleep. When I was fifteen, I decided to quit school and work in the theater on a full-time basis. Besides acting I became involved with the advertising, booking, and staging of the shows.

My favorite role during my teenage years was in a play called *Il Zappatóre*, or, roughly translated, *The Farmer*. It's a story about a peasant farm family who sacrifices to send their son to school in Rome to become a lawyer. When he leaves school as a lawyer, the son is embarrassed about his parents' peasant ways, and he lies to his girlfriend about their real station in life. The family overhears

the lie and throws the son out of the house. Soon thereafter the mother becomes seriously ill. The father goes to Rome and meets with his son at a grand, aristocratic ball. The farmer tells him of his mother's sickness and immediately, facing the loss of his mother, the son repents and reconciles his relationship with his parents. I was about nineteen years old when I played

the part of the son. We staged *Il Zappatóre* in front of many immigrant audiences in Brooklyn. It was a portrayal of what they were going through: Moving away from their country. Leaving family and home. The conflict of learning new ways. It was emotionally charged theater for them and it touched many of their hearts as they sat in a dark Brooklyn theater four thousand miles away from home.

BIG BANDS, SINGERS AND FAVORITE MUSICIANS OFTEN PLAYED THE MANHATTAN BEACH BANDSHELL. THESE WERE POPULAR EVENTS THAT DREW ENORMOUS CROWDS.

J A C K

Actor and comedian

Our family consisted of my parents, one

older and one younger brother, and me, and we lived in

Williamsburg during the surge of prosperity which followed

World War I and during the Depression years. In our neighbor-

hood the difference between those two economic eras was as

invisible as the international date line. The only sign of pros-

perity we had was the loud voice of the Republicans. "Ain't we

got prosperity?" they insisted. It made little difference to us. At

that time someone must have decided that people weren't suffer-

ing enough, so prohibition was invented to *further* increase the

G I L F O R D

burden on the workingman.

My parents separated, and since my father wasn't able to help us financially, my mother worked in a local cloak and suit shop as a "finisher." She was pretty flashy with the needle. She was also pretty sharp about ways to make ends meet. She used to say that hunger embarrassed her, especially in children, more especially in her own children. Some people, she said, believed in Christianity or Judaism or capitalism. She believed in Not Starving. So she was always on the lookout for a way to increase her small income.

One day at the shop, while she was "finishing" with her rapierlike needle and the presser was pounding and gliding his hissing steam iron over the scorched canvas, he recited a recipe for my mother. This was not a formula for making a new kind of cheap no-meat casserole. It was a recipe for a simple mash, a fermentation of potatoes and/or prunes, sugar, and water. With this recipe, he said, it was not only possible but absolutely unavoidable that you would come out with a fairly nonpoisonous whiskey. The presser said he

knew people who were getting rich selling home-brewed whiskey. That got my mother's full attention. Many fine points were discussed. Barrels, space, stirring techniques, and the proper way to cook such a fermentation. They might have been two housewives discussing the best way to make a noodle pudding.

They talked about what kinds of pot you would use to cook this mash. (The recipe began: "Take 100 pounds of prunes...") Where would one buy the ingredients in such large quantities? How could it be done without arousing the suspicions

of the neighbors? Not to mention the cops?

It was decided that a still could be built by a friendly plumber. It would have to fit on my mother's four-burner stove. As for the sugar, potatoes, and prunes, they could be bought in five-pound quantities from various grocers by a little army of consumers enlisted by my mother.

I'll never forget the initial purchase of those items. It was truly a mass buy. In those days, of course, foods were not pre-packed. Almost everything had to be weighed and wrapped on the spot. Potatoes were probably the only thing you'd buy in five-pound bags.

All the cousins, uncles, aunts, and in-laws, and even a few trusted friends, descended on the local grocery stores and literally stripped their shelves of those items. They worked like ants at the height of their buying season. It was probably the greatest hand operation since Pharaoh built the Pyramids with his slaves' bare hands....

The barrel was installed in the bedroom. When the bubbling first started, it sounded like a bathtub full of popcorn popping. As it gained a will of its own, it sounded like a giant pan of ba-con sizzling angrily. This went on for a day and a night. Then it was seeping past the cover and trickling down the sides. The mop and pail were alerted and stationed at the barrel. The next day it literally cascaded over the entire bedroom floor and was heading toward the living room. Had it been liquid it would have

measured a quarter of an inch deep, but it was froth and easily reached the six-inch mark. There we were, fighting to stem the bubbling tide that threatened to engulf us. The presser had told us how to start the bubbles, but, as in the story "Little Pot Boil," he'd neglected to tell us how to turn them off....

During the brewing the reg-ular entrance to our apartment was not used. We had to enter through a side door and all the shades were drawn and we walked on tiptoe. Any unscheduled knock on the door brought a moment of terror, but miraculously no one ever sur-prised us on any of these cook-ins.

Later, when my mother ex-panded the business and was given equal partnership in a larger operation, away from home, she did encounter some surprises that caused us more than a few minutes of agony. One day she was late getting home. Just as we were getting seriously worried, she called us (we were one of the few families in the community to have a phone) and said very calmly, "Look, I've been caught but you are not to worry. Someone is coming to get me out of jail. Just turn the gas a little lower under the soup. I'll be home soon." And she was home in time to serve the soup....

One of our most regular cus-tomers in Brooklyn was a maker of organs, calliopes, and music rolls. He could afford more ex-pensive whiskey than ours, but he preferred my mother's prod-uct. True to her word, she had made a strong, fresh, non-

poisonous whiskey. It was amber (caramel coloring added), had no label, and sold for a reasonable eight dollars a gallon. Our big customer occupied a small house in a section of mostly tenement houses. One entire loft floor was used for testing the music rolls. This went on continuously. He also had a dog with a very large bark. I suppose the competition of the music developed the dog's bark into the loudest noise I ever heard from a domestic animal.

When my mother brought a gallon, she would knock on the downstairs door. The dog would be trying to drown out the mu-sic. My mother would call. It usually took ten minutes to at-tract someone's attention upstairs. One of them would fi-nally yell above the tumult, "Who's there?" My mother would yell back, "The lady from Williamsburg." Then the cus-tomer would let her in, saying "Oh, hello, the lady from Williamsburg." He never knew her name, but the system seemed infallible because even when I would make a delivery, the same music, barking, yelling back and forth, quiet...they'd ask, "Who?" I'd answer, "I'm from the lady from Williamsburg."

RALPH

Editor and photographer

Although they don't hold the distinction

today, for many decades the ports of Brooklyn and Manhattan

were the quintessential heart and soul of New York City. New

York enjoyed the reputation as a natural harbor for maritime

commerce, and Brooklyn played an enormous role as a major

shipping center. The harbor had a vital role in Brooklyn. Be-

sides providing economic growth, it was part of the fabric that

made up Brooklyn's social tapestry. As a kid growing up in Bor-

ough Park, I loved hearing the ships, docked along Brooklyn's

harbor, celebrate the dawning of a new year. It was wonderfully

BROOKLYN WAS KNOWN AS
THE "BOROUGH OF
CHURCHES" BECAUSE OF
THE MANY CHURCH
STEEPLES THAT DOTTED ITS
LANDSCAPE. ONE GREAT WAY
TO CATCH A SUMMER BREEZE
AND ENJOY THE BROOKLYN
VIEW WAS SPENDING AN
EVENING ON A ROOFTOP.

FOLLOWING PAGE: DURING
THE 30S THE STERILIZED
DIAPER SERVICE ON
BROOKLYN'S FOSTER
AVENUE, MADE ITS ROUNDS
PICKING UP BABY DIAPERS.

GINZBURG

exhilarating to hear the deafening blare of the ships' horns every New Year's Eve. The streets of Brooklyn throbbed and resounded with their noise. The yearly ritual in my house was to throw open our windows at the stroke of midnight and listen to the thunderous roar emanating from the freighters docked in Erie Basin, Red Hook, and the piers along Brooklyn Heights. It was a wonderful celebration, a jubilance that defined the important maritime identity of Brooklyn and Manhattan. As wondrous as that celebration was every year, equally enchanting was the sight of the ships themselves. The Bay Ridge Channel served as the entryway for many to the ports in Brooklyn, and often, in addition to the burly commercial freighters and the sleek ocean liners, majestic wooden vessels,

dating from the Revolutionary War, would cruise Brooklyn's waters. During the ferry trips I took with my school class from the 39th Street dock to lower Manhattan, these magnificent ships would loom into view.

The brisk maritime activity attracted many seafaring Scandinavians to Brooklyn, most settling in the Bay Ridge section, which borders 65th Street and 3rd Avenue, and goes north to 8th Avenue. It's a neighborhood situated near the ports, and because of its close proximity to the water, it was a natural place for them to live. During the thirties and forties, it is estimated that more Scandinavians lived in Bay Ridge than in any city in Scandinavia, the majority coming from Norway and Sweden, with a smattering of Danes. Their presence in Bay Ridge added to Brooklyn's cultural mosaic. It

was always great fun to see the Norwegian kids dress in their traditional costumes to celebrate a holiday. Or watch Scandinavian seamen and captains as they walked through the streets. Yet another sign of the Scandinavian culture was the growler, a metal pail used to fetch beer. A typical sight in Bay Ridge was an adolescent running into a saloon and hurrying out with a growler full of beer, usually to a house filled with seamen. Thus, the Scandinavian ritual of "running the growler" was a common event in Bay Ridge.

While the ships cruised the waters, the ubiquitous trolley car played an enormous role on land. Besides serving as ordinary transportation, the trolley car took people to places to explore. One popular excursion was the route to Norton Point, the westernmost point on Coney

Island. As you rode through Coney Island to Norton Point, expanses of farmland, mostly owned and tended by Italian immigrants, came into view. The Italians grew wonderful vegetables—hearty plum tomatoes, eggplants, and peppers. And because the soil was sandy, there was an abundance of root crops—carrots and radishes, for instanc—all fresh and proudly displayed on horse-drawn carts. As the merchants hollered their wares, women scurried to make their purchases, and every sale was assessed on a spring scale that hung from the cart. The prices were noted on the side of a paper bag with a thick, black grease pencil. As part of the selling ritual, before the merchant added his figures, he would first moisten the pencil by lightly jabbing its tip on his tongue.

My apartment building on 47th Street and 9th Avenue was a four-story walk-up with the pretentious name of the Albert Arms. Ironically, every building in the area had a very genteel English name, like the Buckingham or the Royal Arms, yet most of the families who lived in these buildings were barely making ends meet. Amusing as it may sound today, a big status symbol of the time was the elevator. If a family lived in an apartment building that was serviced by an elevator, they were looked upon as a family that was doing rather well. Whether you lived in an elevator building or not, during a hot August evening, people would escape to the roofs of their buildings hoping to cool off with

a summer breeze. From a rooftop's vantage point, Brooklyn's landscape was quite beautiful and inspiring. Standing atop my building, a diverse collection of church steeples, loftily jutting into the summer sky, shimmered in the late evening sun. Known then as the Borough of Churches, Brooklyn had very few buildings higher than six stories, with the notable exception

of the Williamsburg Savings Bank. The steeples dotted the landscape as far as the eye could see.

P.S. 160 on Fort Hamilton Parkway and 51st Street was a wonderful school where the kids were taught by a strict staff of Irish teachers. Most of the teachers were women and almost all were "Miss." Since all the buildings were coal heated, a popular digression for the boys

was watching the heating coal being delivered to the school. During my earlier years at P.S. 160 the coal was delivered by horse and cart, which eventually gave way to trucks. The coal trucks stood atop tires constructed of hard rubber and those tires made the most peculiar sound, a cackling of sorts, as they rolled along the street. The men on the coal truck, grimy and dirty in their navy blue overalls, would set up a wooden duct from the hatch of the truck to the coal bin of the school. As the truck's hatch titled, the coal would tumble out, its progress somberly assisted by the shovel-wielding men. Although the adults knew this work was the dregs of labor, most of the male students perceived the coal men as symbols of cool masculinity and looked upon them as heroes.

On those occasions when I give a speech

or address a banquet, I usually preface the talk by mentioning some biographical data, often commenting that I was born in Brooklyn. It's uncanny how often I hear an enthusiastic smattering of applause when I mention my native borough. I'm fascinated when this happens, because many times these speeches are given in distant places around the country, thousands of miles away from my birthplace, including places outside the United States. Not surprisingly, the two areas that give the loudest ovations are Florida and California, two states that are second homes

Former U.S. Attorney for the Southern District in New York.

RUDOLPH GIULIANI

to many native Brooklynites.

Although both my parents are of Italian ancestry, their families came from different regions in Italy. Their playful debates and sermons about which province offered more to humanity, made things quite interesting around the house on Hawthorne Street in Flatbush. My father's family came from northern Italy, near Florence, "where they speak perfect Italian," as he would say. My mother, on the other hand, descended from a family that lived near Naples, argued how southern Italy "was the land of warm, friendly people made famous by Italian singers like the great Caruso." They spent hours deliberating about their ancestry, teasing each other in good fun. In addition to the ancestral comparisons, another bone of contention was the baseball teams each rooted for. Because my dad was born and raised in Manhattan, his allegiance was to the Yankees. Mom, like the rest of her family, all native Brooklynites, was a Dodger fan. The discussions about which was the better baseball team went on nonstop.

As funny as it may seem, my sense of individuality may have been rooted by the fact that my dad raised me a Yankee fan in Brooklyn. One of my earliest memories is my father dressing me up in a Yankee uniform and sending me out to play. As soon as I went outside, several neighborhood boys came over and threw me into some mud. I went home terribly upset, but my father sent me outside again. He

was determined that I learn to stand up for what I believed in. My father and I were constantly being teased and looked upon as traitors, especially on the days when we traveled to the Bronx to see the Yankees play. My mother's family and our neighbors just couldn't understand why, because we lived several blocks away from Ebbets Field, we had to travel all that distance to see a Yankee game. And on those occasions when the whole family got together, it was important that I was prepared for the ensuing arguments with my Dodger-loving cousins and uncles about comparative batting averages, ERAs and slugging percentages. My interest in debate and learning how to prepare for an argument undoubtedly stemmed from these discussions.

When she graduated from high school, my mother's ambition was to become a schoolteacher. Unfortunately, due to a slight respiratory ailment, she didn't pass the physical requirement, so she eventually moved into other jobs, which paid more than the teaching profession. Her passion to teach continued, however, so when I was born I became her sole pupil. Even before she enrolled me into a Brooklyn elementary school, my mother began teaching me arithmetic, literature, and history, spending hours on each subject. She created an environment where learning was an enjoyable endeavor, so by the time I began my formal schooling, I had developed an attitude of enjoying the learning process. History

was my favorite subject because I was, and still am, fascinated to learn about how people lived, where they came from, and why they did things a certain way.

Although we moved to Garden City, Long Island, several years later, I returned to Brooklyn for my high-school education. Bishop Laughlin High School at that time was one of the best schools in the Catholic educational system. It was a scholarship school that was available to students in all the Catholic parishes of New York's five boroughs, as well as those in the Nassau and Suffolk counties of Long Island. To qualify for Bishop Laughlin, a student needed to pass an entrance examination. Usually only one or two students per parish were accepted. My years at Bishop Laughlin were filled with wonderful academic experiences. The school's teaching staff was comprised of Christian Brothers, a Catholic order that stressed discipline in behavior and academic work. There were several occasions when I was punished for bad behavior, but the brothers exacted their discipline in a way that suggested a genuine caring on their part.

My second-year music teacher at Bishop Laughlin was a very inspiring instructor. He was an excellent teacher who was able to effectively share his passion for opera with his students. He'd play excerpts from operas or classical music and then elucidate each act or movement. On the weekdays leading into the Saturday afternoon *Texaco Opera* broadcast, he would

distribute an outline of that Saturday's opera and explain the story in its entirety. The last thing most of us sophomores wanted to do was to watch an opera on a weekend afternoon. But one day, after listening to Handel's *Julius Caesar* and Tchaikovsky's *1812* Overture, I got hooked and began supplementing my rock 'n' roll 45s, with a collection of Italian operas. My interest in opera heightened to a point where I began to record performances off the radio, attended opera performances, and started an opera club at Bishop Laughlin. As they say in the law profession, my music teacher was the "proximate cause" for my lifelong passion for opera.

BATTLESHIP MAX COHN ON SANDS STREET WAS THE OUTFITTER FOR MANY NAVY YARD OFFICERS.

Actor

OVERLEAF: THE FUN HOUSE AT STEEPLECHASE PARK FEATURED ITS POPULAR FLOOR BLOWER THAT CAUGHT MANY A VISITOR BY SURPRISE.

I was thrilled when I got a summer job

working as a short-order cook on the Coney Island boardwalk. The thought of working near my friends, many of whom had found work at Nathan's, Hebrew National, Howard Johnson's, the bowling alley, the movie theaters, or the ice-cream and game stands that dotted the beachfront, was an exciting prospect. We all knew each other from the neighborhood or high school, so there was bound to be lots of fun. I was also excited because I looked forward to working alongside Tootsie. Tootsie was an oversized man who was known as the best hot-dog and ham-

LOU GOSSETT, JR.

burger cook in Coney Island. He was a wonderful character who had a penchant for attracting customers to his stand. As soon as he opened for business, Tootsie would go into his hawking routine, bellowing in a baritone voice, "Hey, get 'em while they're hot!" He'd bark that phrase from early morning to late at night, while at the same time flipping a row of sizzling, blistering burgers faster than anyone on the beach. While he was a colorful, fun-loving character with great pizzazz, he was serious about his cooking. He prided himself as a conscientious cook who never sacrificed quality for speed, so his griddle creations were always cooked to perfection.

The appetizing tastes and smells of the food I ate in Brooklyn made a lasting impression. I was raised the only child of Lou and Helen Gossett, and because they both worked, many afternoons were spent with my maternal grandmother in Sheepshead Bay. Living with my grandmother was *her* mother, a former slave who lived to be 117 years old. I loved watching those two women in the kitchen as they prepared wonderful dinners on a stove heated by wood and coal. They were used to cooking with wood and coal because that's how they were taught in the South. Despite the urban surroundings, my grandmother's backyard was full of chickens. I can still hear the clucking and squawking of those chickens, which my grandmother occasionally slaughtered for dinner. She and my great-grandmother spent hours creat-

ing the most delectable Southern dishes, cooking up specialties that included flavorful smoked meats, smoked turkey, mustard greens, and fried chicken. Although some of the food looked terribly unpleasant at first glance, it always tasted terrific and fresh.

On weekends my father worked his second job, as a first mate on a fishing boat docked in Sheepshead Bay. He and a buddy would sail early on a Saturday or Sunday morning, and bring home a fresh catch of fish. Because of the diversity of his catches, I learned to eat all kinds of seafood. The savory smell of fish frying in a skillet, seasoned in a variety of ways, permeated our Brooklyn apartment. Whatever we couldn't eat, my father would pickle or give away to families in the neighborhood that didn't have much. I once got the bright idea of going out with my dad on one of his fishing excursions. After an excruciating day of seasickness, I returned home vowing never to step on a boat again. As I got older, however, I came to love the ocean and fishing.

We lived at 2832 West 35th Street, right across the street from P.S. 188. When I entered the world at Coney Island Hospital, I was part of the first generation of Gossetts to be born in the North. My father's folks came from South Carolina and the Bahamas and my mother's family traced their roots to Georgia. The experiences that the early Gossetts had in Brooklyn were positive and supportive, thanks in large part to

the people in Coney Island. In those days there was a sense of caring for one's neighbor, and a value system that included reaching out to people in need. My father experienced this caring soon after he came north as a teenager. He arrived in Brooklyn at a young age and got a job working the big newsstand at the last stop of the Coney Island line. When his family fell on hard times, his brothers and sisters were immediately placed in foster homes. Because he was the oldest in the family, he continued to work, desperately trying to avoid a similar fate. Nevertheless, the local foster agency began pressuring him to move into the foster home and give up his job. When Rocco Silvestri, his boss at the newsstand, heard about my father's situation, he immediately stepped in. He adopted my father, telling the authorities that he'd take full responsibility for his actions. The word spread through the neighborhood about my father's plight, and soon many neighbors lent support. Even the ominous-looking gangsters, regular customers at the newsstand, did their part. They would often slip my father some extra money to make ends meet.

When I grew up in Brooklyn, I found similar experiences. The protective umbrella that us Coney Island kids grew up under in the 1940s was the network of concerned mothers who kept constant watch in the neighborhood. God forbid if a kid stepped out of line. The mothers would alert the trouble-maker's family and the problem was immediately rectified. In those days, Coney Island was predominantly Jewish, yet every kid was looked after, regardless of race or color. The teaching staff in the schools were equally caring and protective. There was an incredible core of teachers at Mark Twain Junior High School that adopted us like we were their own. Many of the teachers lived in the neighborhood and their children went to the same school. It wasn't surprising to hear your parents say they met your teacher in the supermarket, the dry cleaners, or at religious services. Because of this kindred spirit, few students failed. Indeed, most thrived. It was a high-school English teacher, Mr. Gustave Blum, who got me interested in acting. Blum pushed me to audition for a Broadway lead in a show called *Take a Giant Step*. It turned out to be the biggest step I ever took. I went to the audition on a whim and won the part.

The success I enjoyed playing Broadway made me a celebrity in high school. My last year at Abraham Lincoln High School turned out to be really special. Not only was I a Broadway star, I was also senior-class president. The worldly perspective I thought I possessed, however, came crashing down the night of the Lincoln senior prom. After escorting my date to the prom, we hurried off to listen to some jazz at Birdland, topping that off with a late snack at the House of Chan. As my date and I settled in, I triumphantly ordered dinner. Feeling like a million bucks, I was polishing off my rack of ribs when suddenly the waiter brought out two finger bowls of water with a wedge of lemon in each bowl. My date, as confused as I was, asked me what kind of delicacy this course was. Ever playing the role of the bon vivant, and trying to mask my own bewilderment, I authoritatively explained it was a special type of Chinese soup. So we began to spoon it down. I made matters worse by telling her to flavor the soup with sugar, my experienced palate suggesting it needed additional spicing. Needless to say, many of our companion diners, as well as the waiters serving us, all broke out laughing. It was a humbling, yet learning experience for the Broadway star from Abraham Lincoln High School.

J O S É

Dancer

It was June 1928—I was nine—when the

big letter came. My father had become a naturalized U.S. cit-

izen, thereby making his children U.S. citizens automatically.

More important, he was ready for us to come. He'd even sent a

special dress for my sister Norina and a flannel suit for me to

wear when we landed in New York. Our little family packed up

and headed for Naples, on the opposite coast of Italy, where we

were to depart for the United States. . . . I don't remember much

about that boat trip, but I remember my first impression of New

York, as we docked at one of that city's West Side piers, then

G R E C O

came down the gangplank. It was terrifying.

All around us were skyscrapers that dwarfed even the largest buildings in Naples. The sidewalks were mobbed with people, more people than I'd ever thought existed. All the background noise—the blend of rumbling trucks, angry taxi horns, and roaring elevated trains—made me fear for my life.

And then, up in front of us, I saw a handsome man, looking debonair in his straw hat. He was smiling at us and hurrying in our direction. He was my father. He looked like a god.

As he reached us, he threw his arms around me joyously and kissed me and flung me into the air. Then he did the same with my sister. And finally, he embraced my mother, holding her

for the longest time.

My father arranged for our trunks to be put into a taxi. While they were being loaded, he turned toward me and reached into his pocket. He pulled out a fifty-cent piece and four dimes.

"Here, Costanzo," he said. "This is fifty cents and this is forty cents. But this is one coin and this is four coins. Which would you like, the fifty-cent piece or the four dimes?"

Well, I wasn't stupid. I could count. "I like the little ones," I said, choosing the dimes. I'll never forget that. My father smiled broadly and poured the dimes into my hand. Then he gave the fifty-cent piece to my sister. Then we all climbed into the cab and started off.

We were headed toward Brooklyn, toward Hopkinson Avenue, where my father was

boarding with my mother's brother and his wife.

Even with my entire family beside me, the taxi ride from Manhattan to Brooklyn was a harrowing experience. The traffic, the astonishing hustle and bustle of the city, and the incredible noise was almost more than I could bear. . . .

But once we got over the Brooklyn Bridge—I was too frightened to be much impressed with it—things began to change. The buildings were smaller, the noise level lower. The cars in the street and the people on the sidewalks seemed to move more slowly. . . .

We stayed at the house on Hopkinson Avenue for about six months, during which time I never heard a happy word between either my aunt and my uncle or my aunt and my father. She was impossibly bitter. About what, I shall never know. Perhaps it was the way of southern puritanical women.

But it wasn't all bad for me. I had three cousins to play with, and there were other children nearby. And my father often took us to the Canarsie Beach, or Coney Island.

One August day, Papa had us all dress up in our best clothing—me in the suit he'd sent me in Montorio, Mama in her fur-collared coat (despite the heat), Norina in her Sunday finest. Papa even put on a vest for the occasion.

Then we all went to the photographer's shop on Fulton Street, next to the Paragon Theater. "My family is together now," my father said, "and I want never to forget it." We spent more than an hour with the photographer, who impressed me as being a nice man.

During the week I saw very little of my father. He spent his days as a laborer on the IND subway, helping to build the part of the line that runs through Brooklyn.

And I also spent some of my summer at work helping a Montorio *paisano* who owned a shoe repair shop, painting the edges of the new soles and heels black. His language brought Montorio back to me, which helped relieve my loneliness.

The neighborhood we lived in was a bad one (though not nearly as bad as it is today, I am afraid). But I was innocent of such things for awhile. One afternoon, my father came home with a gift for me, a scooter. I fell in love with it immediately. I rode it everywhere, even to the shoe shop.

One day, after work, I went to get my scooter, which I'd left outside at the curb. It was gone. I searched for it, thinking I must have put it somewhere else, but it was nowhere to be seen. Then the horrible truth dawned on me: My scooter had been stolen.

I remember sitting down on the curb and crying. It wasn't simply the loss of the scooter, devastating though that was. It was also the realization of how cruel people could be....

We soon moved to a better neighborhood, still in Brooklyn, taking a house on Herkimer Street, and I transferred to P.S. 155. By that time, I'd caught up with my proper grade—fourth—

since I was learning English quickly....

I continued to have a hard time in school, not only with my classmates, but also with my teachers. I remember one particularly painful incident that took place when I was in the fourth grade.

I was sitting in class, doing my best to read my book, when I heard fire engines outside. Now, I had never seen a fire engine, not in real life. But shortly before, I'd seen a movie about a

fire, in which the firemen, riding their engines, were my heroes. Since I was at an impressionable age, this had struck my mind.

Hearing the engines and clanging bells, I got excited. I jumped up from my seat and started shouting *i pompieri, i pompieri!* (the firemen, the firemen!). Everyone in the class burst out laughing, and I was ridiculed and shamed.

My teacher, a very vicious person, came over to me with

fury in her eyes and a ruler in her hands. "Stick out your hands," she said.

I did. And she whacked me with the ruler with such force that she cut my fingers. I still have the scars—and all because I interrupted the class for a moment....

When Mama came home, she told me that there was nothing she could do, that I'd just have to take it. So I did. And I decided never again to open my mouth in class. I went into my

own world.

That world was one of glamour, excitement, and beauty. It was a world of Hollywood, of the movies, of Valentino. For me, the place of fantasy was the Paragon Theatre, on Fulton Street.

DESIGNED BY JOHN A. ROEBLING, AND OPENING IN 1883, THE BROOKLYN BRIDGE IS A MAGNIFICENT BLEND OF ART AND ENGINEERING THAT PLAYS AN ENORMOUS PART IN BROOKLYN CULTURE.

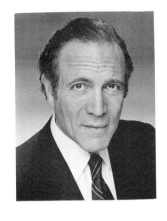

Actor

Mr. Brown was an unusual character living

in the early fifties society of Brooklyn. He was the sole reminder

of rural Midwood, a symbol of the days when corn and wheat

grew on Brooklyn soil, instead of six-story apartment buildings

and urban playgrounds. In the shadow of my apartment building

at 1270 East 18th Street between Avenue L and Avenue M,

Farmer Brown, as the kids called him, tended religiously to his

farm. It was a small parcel of land, maybe an acre, and his crops

included corn and tomatoes, as well as eggs from his clucking

chickens. He was a stern and stoic man, always outfitted in his

DAVID
GROH

blue overalls, and during hot summer evenings he'd stand on his property and stare dispassionately at passersby. Farmer Brown recognized change was on the horizon in Brooklyn, progress that included noisy car traffic disrupting his quiet and apartment buildings that cut off his sunlight. He was quietly outraged at the change, but at the same time, knew it was inevitable. Except for the days when he sold his crops to the neighbors, he rarely spoke to anyone, preferring instead to insulate himself from the encroaching world.

Around the corner from Mr. Brown's farm was a black-asphalted neighborhood playground. Adjoining my apartment building, the playground was home to the neighborhood punchball and stickball games. Without a doubt, the best punchball hitter in the neighborhood was Marty Weingarten. He was several years older than most of the gang, so maybe his extra strength helped. Whatever it was, Marty punched a ball farther than anyone on the block. The big achievement for most kids was hitting the apartment building wall on a fly, a feat that took years to attain. Marty could punch shots that hit the wall every time, and on special occasions he'd blast shots beyond the wall where it slanted into a courtyard. The amazing thing was, the courtyard was surrounded by a twenty-foot cyclone fence, so for a spaldeen to clear that fence, it had to be hit very high as well as long. The kids in the neighborhood were so in awe of Marty's accomplishments they nicknamed the building courtyard "The Weingarten."

I was a better student than an athlete, particularly excelling in mathematics and sciences. My father was an architect, a good reason why I displayed such aptitude in those subjects. During my years at P.S. 193, Hudde Junior High School, and Brooklyn Tech, I was a studious and introverted student who nevertheless got along with the rest of the class. While stamp and comic-book collecting were my favorite indoor activities, I loved being outside with the rest of the boys. One summer a polio outbreak regrettably put an end to all outdoor activities. Several of the kids in the neighborhood fell victim to the disease, which provoked a genuine scare among the mothers. Salk had yet to discover the vaccine for polio, so the preventive measure was to keep the children inside. It was agonizing to spend the summer indoors. My parents tried to soften the pain, buying my sister and me extra toys like Erector Sets, dolls, and model airplanes, but nonetheless being held captive all summer was a dreadful experience. At the time we didn't understand what all the fuss was about.

The rare times we were allowed out that summer were for mundane things like haircuts. The neighborhood was full of warm and wonderful characters, and one of the most popular among the kids was Vito G. DeLuna, the local barber. Vito was proud of that middle initial G. and his immaculate barbershop, which was scented by a crispy-clean fragrance that permeated the air. He was an Italian immigrant who'd recount fascinating stories about his old country, as well as patriotically expound on the greatness of America. Sitting in his large leather barber chair, I listened fondly to his enchanting stories, and as he continued to tell his tales, this warm, colorful man grew larger than life. When you left the shop it was important to him that you say, "Good-bye, Vito G. DeLuna," always remembering to stress the G.

In addition to playing sports in the playground, another favorite activity was fishing. With a couple of friends, I'd hop onto the Green Bus Line with my fishing rod and travel to the Rockaways, Jamaica Bay, or the Steeplechase Pier. Depending on the season, we'd come home with a great catch of blues, fluke, porgies, blackfish, or bass. My fishing buddies and I were extremely excited the day we learned about a program sponsored by the Sheepshead Bay Boat Owners Association. During July and August, a kid could spend a whole day on a fishing boat absolutely free! All that was necessary was a signed release from your mother. We jumped at this grand opportunity and spent many summer days on fishing expeditions. On a couple of occasions we even made money on the deal. We'd take turns watering our catch, so by the time we got back to land, our fish were still flipping. We'd walk off the boat and people waiting to buy fresh fish would be standing on the dock. When they saw our fish flipping, they'd ask, "You have fresh fish, kid?" We'd tell them it was the freshest on the boat, so we never had a problem selling our catch. The price was right, too, usually two fish for a dollar. While we became popular with our customers on the dock, the mates on the boat came to resent our little enterprise.

URBAN PROGRESS TOOK THE FORM OF MULTI-LEVEL SUBWAY CONSTRUCTION DURING THE 1920S.

BUDDY

I cherished Sunday mornings in

Brooklyn. I eagerly looked forward to the rousing softball and

touch football games my friends and I played against the other

kids in the neighborhood. It was a great release. Most of the time

during the week was spent working or going to school. There

were a variety of jobs I held. I worked in a liquor store, a groc-

ery, dry cleaners, drugstore, or with my father in his upholstery

business. I even worked for a doctor at night, answering his

telephone. I was born on Kosciusko Street in the Williamsburg

section, but soon after moved to 1379 54th Street in Borough

Comedian

HACKETT

Park. I attended P.S. 103 and
from there went to New Utrecht
High School. The best memories
I have about Brooklyn were the
years I was just starting to work
in show business, right after
World War II ended, from 1946
until television became popular.
The Friday entertainment page
in the *New York Daily Mirror*
would advertise twenty to thirty
nightclubs listed under
BROOKLYN. These were the places
guys like me played, guys who
were doing comedy, still trying
to break in. On nights I played,
the boys in the neighborhood
would all pile in their cars and
come to watch my routine. Their
support kept me working,
because if a comedian could
draw people into a club, he was
asked back. The encouragement
I got from my friends and the
number of clubs available to
hone my act was very important.
The variety of places to play in
Brooklyn far surpassed those
found in other parts of the
country. Detroit had two or three
clubs, Chicago maybe four or
five. But Brooklyn had an
abundance of clubs. There were
some places where you worked
one night and others you'd play
four nights a week. Some you
worked every weekend. I learned
my trade and polished my craft
at these clubs.

SURF AVENUE AND STRATTON
HENDERSON WALK WAS A POPULAR
CORNER IN CONEY ISLAND DURING
THE 1930S.

Singer

I grew up in the Bedford-Stuyvesant area

in Brooklyn, first living on Dean Street, and eventually settling

into my grandmother's house on Howard and Hancock. Bedford-

Stuyvesant was a friendly, middle-class neighborhood, where

working-class people from all different nationalities, colors and

religions lived side by side. I hung around kids from all types of

ethnic backgrounds and shared their same problems, especially

dealing with our old-world parents who couldn't understand

their newly "Americanized" kids. Our fascination with a newly

developed, electronic gizmo called television, and later, rock 'n'

RICHIE
HAVENS

roll, alienated us from the older generation. Our common struggle pulled us together as we fought to claim our new American identity, one that was based on a different culture from our parents'.

My grandmother's house was typical of the family unit representative of that era—three generations all living under one roof. My father worked as an electroplater and he'd seek relief from his travails when he came home by reading books or playing music with his brother. There were many nights he'd come home, open the piano, and sing songs, drink beer, and have a grand old time. He was a fine musician who never took a lesson, instead learning all the melodies by ear. I inherited his musical ability, especially the gift to hear music for the very first time and repeat it back verbatim. I particularly liked to show off this talent in Mrs. Dufor's seventh-grade music class at P.S. 26. As part of her lessons, she would play a musical passage and the class would have to hum it back. After going around the class, usually to no avail, she counted on me to get it right. "Okay, Richie," she would say, "let's hear it the right way." On cue, I would proudly repeat the passage. While my proficiency endeared me with Mrs. Dufor, many of my fellow students didn't appreciate my showing them up.

While my father was mercurial and tempestuous, my mother was a quiet, fair-minded person. She made it a point not to favor any of her children, so

much so that it almost was comical in retrospect. I remember Sunday afternoons during the summer in which the family would take a walk in the park. My brothers and sister and I would all be dressed in exactly the same outfits, little sailor suits, as we walked along with my parents and grandparents.

Although my parents played an important role in my life, the person who made the biggest impact was my grandmother. Because my father worked days and my mother worked nights, I saw my grandmother more than anyone else. She had a dominant personality cultivated from a strict British education on the island of Barbados. My first years in school were absolutely humiliating because of her strong British influence. I was forced to go to school in knickers and argyle socks. You can't imagine the teasing I was subjected to during those days. Here was this little black kid, in the middle of Bedford-Stuyvesant, attending classes at P.S. 26 dressed in this getup. After several years of abuse, I begged my mother for regular clothes, which she finally agreed to only after receiving my grandmother's blessing.

My grandmother was an extremely religious person, a Methodist by faith, and a Christian by application. I remember seeing her give away my grandfather's clothes to several men in the neighborhood, or inviting some poor people into the house for a hot supper. She lived the sayings of the Bible. Every Sunday before the family went to

church, she held a service in her bedroom. She would first call in my parents, aunts, and uncles and lead prayers with them, and then she would call in me, my brothers, sister, and cousins, and lead prayers with us. She would ask God for things that we could relate to: "Please help this family down the street." "Please watch over our uncle in the Army"—prayers for things we saw needed improvement. She was leading a life the way Jesus Christ asks us to lead our lives, and I thought it appropriate that December 25 was her birthday. I was thirteen years old when she died, and I was totally blown away by her death. She meant so much to me that still having my parents was little consolation. I had grown up under her wing. Watching my parents being guided by her showed me where the real power and strength had been.

About the same time my grandmother passed away, Bedford-Stuyvesant began to change from a middle-class community to a poverty-stricken neighborhood. The people who lived there began their move to the suburbs while many oppressed Southern blacks began coming north for jobs. Those that eventually settled in Brooklyn found bad conditions. The poverty and hopelessness of the situation contributed to the deterioration of the neighborhood.

By this time, I was becoming more disillusioned at my education from Franklin K. Lane high school, and the street-gang and police violence that was going on along Jefferson Avenue. I took a

Western Union messenger job that only made things worse. As a new recruit I was given the responsibility of delivering death messages to people when they answered their doors. Many times, as soon as they opened their door, their faces would crinkle up in abject fear, knowing full well bad news was to follow. I walked away from that job after two years, but it did give me a perspective on just how fragile the human condition is.

One of the best remembrances I have of Brooklyn is the beauty of the sky and clouds there. As a kid, I would hike up a hilltop in Highland Park or into a neighboring cemetery, and lie down on the soft, green grass, cup my hands around my eyes to block everything else from view, and look up into the expanse overhead. After a while, big, white, puffy clouds would float into view and I would frame this beautiful vista of these stark white clouds suspended against the golden blue sky for hours on end.

ON A TYPICAL WEEKEND DURING THE TURN OF THE CENTURY, GENTLEMEN USED BICYCLES AND HORSE AND BUGGIES TO MAKE THEIR WAY AROUND PROSPECT PARK.

I grew up in Coney Island in a two-story

house on Ocean Parkway, in a neighborhood mainly comprised

of Jewish families. My father was a lawyer and my mother taught

Russian language and literature at Brooklyn College. It was an

New York City comptroller

environment that strongly encouraged the value of education,

work, and religion. There were many relatives living in the area,

FOLLOWING PAGES: IN 1934, FARMER JOHN MAZROVECK SHOWED OFF HIS PRIZE PIG ON HIS FARM AT STANLEY AVENUE AND JEROME STREET IN THE EASTERN SECTION OF BROOKLYN. BROOKLYN'S BOROUGH HALL UNDERGOING RENOVATION IN 1949.

so there were lots of people around to keep an eye on me and my

twin brother when my parents were away from the house. The

person that we spent the most time with was my grandfather, who

lived in the upstairs apartment. He treated me and my brother

ELIZABETH HOLTZMAN

109

as equals, never showing favoritism. It was a ritual to spend early mornings with him. My brother and I would quietly crawl upstairs to his apartment while our parents were sleeping. He'd give us breakfast, ask us to recite our arithmetic tables or inquire about a lesson in school, then send us back down before our parents awoke. We enjoyed his company and all the things we did together. I especially looked forward to the ferry rides from Sheepshead Bay. On a crystal-clear, beautiful summer day he would take us on the ferry that ran from Sheepshead Bay to Rockaway. We'd spend what seemed like the whole day ferrying back and forth, and when we grew bored and tired, he'd take us home.

At the end of our school day at P.S. 153, we would go to Hebrew class. We'd breathe a sigh of relief when we didn't encounter the neighborhood bully on our way home. He had a particular anger against Jewish kids so the route home from Hebrew school was his favorite territory. When we did get home in good order, the remainder of the afternoon was spent doing homework or playing outside. On the next block was a sandlot that we converted into a ball field and on the days we weren't playing ball, we would walk down to the house where a family had a chicken coop and listen to the chickens squawk and cluck. While I participated in many of the outdoor activities, I particularly enjoyed art and astronomy. My adolescent dream was that someday I would be an artist. To satisfy these ambitions, I asked my parents to be enrolled in an art class. My mother accompanied me to art school, but after a short while, even I realized art wasn't a strong aptitude. It wasn't a major disappointment because soon thereafter I took up the piano, which I played through high school. It seemed I was better suited for the piano because I eventually reached a proficiency of giving several recitals.

Some of my best memories of Brooklyn were the years I attended Abraham Lincoln High School. The quality and professionalism of the teachers there was superb and their commitment to the students absolute. During the early years of the Depression, many well-qualified people who had lost their private-sector jobs accepted teaching positions in the New York City school system. It was a good-paying job that offered security. They approached their subject, whether it was history, English, or mathematics, with great zeal. The school also offered a rich program of extracurricular activities. It promoted active participation by the students, and consequently many of them got involved and committed themselves to a broad range of activities. I always participated in some activity, whether it was the sing or student government. One year my brother decided to run for class president and asked me to run as vice president. We mustered a support group made up of art students who fashioned posters and banners and also dreamed

up a catchy campaign slogan: "Win with the Twins!" We went on to win that race and celebrated our victory with a party in the backyard, which, much to my parents' chagrin, was plowed under by the happy campaign revelers.

In many ways, growing up in Brooklyn in the forties was comparable to living in a small town in America. There was a great feeling of support in the neighborhood, and most of the families, shopkeepers, civil servants, and children knew each

other. There was a great sense of pride for the neighborhood. My parents often spoke of the wonderful opportunity there was in this country. They instilled in us a sense of someday giving something back to the city. In my younger days I never aspired to be a government worker, but as I grew older that inner sense eventually surfaced. It is those values, which I learned from my parents, grandparents, and teachers in Brooklyn, that motivates me today.

RED

*Head coach
of the New York Knicks
championship basketball
teams (1969–70
and 1972–73)*

OVERLEAF: IN THE SHADOW
OF THE SKYSCRAPERS OF
MANHATTAN, BROOKLYN
BECAME KNOWN AS THE
WORKING MAN'S BOROUGH.

I was born on the Lower East Side of Man-

hattan on August 10, 1920, and moved to Brooklyn with my

family when I was four years old. It was as though we had moved

to the country. The neighborhood was mostly Italians and Jews.

We lived in the Ocean Hill-Brownsville section on the third floor

of a tenement at 2110 Atlantic Avenue off Saratoga Avenue. In

those days you could come home at two or three in the morning

and still feel safe.... I was out in the streets all the time, playing

ball, while my brother, Julie, was dutifully working. My playing

ball didn't go over too big with my parents. Uncle Leon was

HOLZMAN

something of a sports fan, but my father had no interest in games except for soccer. He worked very hard just to keep things going....

The extended family unit was our main source of entertainment. Friends were always dropping by, asking, "What time do we eat?"

Sunday afternoons were a popular time for visiting. Loads of people would come by, have a big, satisfying meal, some wine, look for a bed or their favorite nook, and take a nap. Our home looked like a dormitory on Sunday afternoons.

One of the closest friends of the family was Morris Barth, who was only about five feet tall but worth his weight in gold. Morris was an expert in *schtelen bonkers*, the art of placing glass cups with alcohol in them on your body. Morris would heat the cups and draw out a cold or a fever. In those days people would go to the beach with *bonkers* (cup marks) all over them, and you knew they had gone through the treatment....

After a couple of years of living in the tenement, we moved around the corner to a place above a butcher shop at 299 Saratoga Avenue. There was no air-conditioning, and on summer nights with the windows open in my bedroom I was able to get a hell of an education. Back then relatives often all lived together and not always in harmony. Fist fights, sexual squabbling, bickering over money, gossip—I heard it all, with the choicest of street language thrown in for good measure.

One guy named Schnitz would come home about three in the morning every Saturday and wake up the whole neighborhood singing: "Why did I have to get married to that ball 'n chain. My wife is a stone-hearted jailer, and she treats all the men the same." Around the corner from where I lived was St. Clair McEllway school. I quickly became a schoolyard rat there, playing soccer, football, handball, softball, baseball, and especially basketball.

My father was always concerned about me making the wrong friends. "Pop," I excitedly described one of my new acquaintances, "this guy is cool." In my father's mind the word *cool* must have made him think the guy was doing something he should not be doing. "Roita"— that was his Yiddish word for Red—"*Vere is dere kool? Luzmur him zayn.*" (Translated: "Where is the cool—let me see him.") My father wanted to check him out.

Yiddish was all we spoke for many years at home and I really loved the sound of the language, with its colorful and not quite translatable expressions. *Narishket* (foolishness) was a word my parents used to describe my ball playing....

After a while I became so good at sports that I spent all my time playing ball. My parents wanted me to study. I wanted to play ball. Some nights, in order to play at the neighborhood center, I would have to throw my shoes and equipment out the back window of our apartment and then fumble around in the dark in the courtyard searching

for them....

The first organized sport I became interested in was soccer. My father and my Uncle Leon would take me every Sunday to the Polo Grounds or Hawthorne Field in Brooklyn. Even if it was raining or bitter cold or a blizzard, we would always go. My uncle had the car—one year he even had a Nash open touring car with a running board. A highlight of that time was watching the Hakoah All Stars—a great professional soccer team from Vienna—at the Polo Grounds.

My uncle was a New York Giants fan living in Brooklyn, and although I liked the Dodgers, he converted me to rooting for the Giants....But of all the sports, basketball was the one I liked best. My uncle Leon would take me to see the Brooklyn Jewels play at Arcadia Hall on Halsey Street in the Bushwick section of Brooklyn. The Jewels had been the St. John's "Wonder Five" and had all turned pro together, joining the American League....

Mac Kinsbrunner was the star of the Jewels, and he was a master dribbler who could control the ball all night. I sat in the stands and studied his every move. And for a week after that I would be Kinsbrunner as I tried out what I had seen him do on anybody I could get to play against me.

Another basketball team that I went out of my way to see was the Harlem Renaissance Five, known as the Rens. An all-black team, they played on Sunday nights in the Renaissance Casino nightclub in Harlem and used to come to Arcadia Hall to go against the Jewels.

The Rens, founded by Bob Douglas in 1922, were unlike the Harlem Globetrotters, who were more show business than basketball. For that time there was probably no better basketball team in the world than the Rens. From 1932 to 1936 they won 473 games against just 49 losses. They played one-night stands and traveled and slept in their own custom-made "ten-thousand-dollar bus." Games were played on unfamiliar courts against town teams who hired the refs, and often they would be very physical. But the Rens played so many games that they knew each other's moves instinctively. They played a switching man-to-man defense to save extra steps and conserve energy and emphasized team basketball and unselfishness. Their style made a big impression on me and I filed it away for future reference.

Singer

I was born in a small lying-in hospital in

Brooklyn...on June 30, 1917. I've been told that the nurses

exhibited me all over the place, terribly enthused and surprised

about my copper color. Since my dad, whose fine copper glow I

inherited, was hung up in a card game where he was earning the

money to pay the hospital bill and did not appear until much

later, I'm convinced there was more sheer surprise than enthusi-

asm in the attitude of the nurses.... The world into which I was

born, the one which exerted the strongest pull on my person-

ality, was a small, tight world, one which many people, white and

L E N A
H O R N E

Negro, are unaware existed early in this century. It was the world of the Negro middle class. Our family, I find, followed most of the patterns that sociologists—those few who have studied the so-called bourgeoisie—have found were common to our class. We were isolated from the mainstream of Negro life, seeing a relatively narrow group of people. For example, I'm told it was characteristic of our class not to be Baptists or Methodists, which most Negroes were then. We were not. I was baptized, but not confirmed, in the Catholic faith; and my grandmother (Cora Calhoune Horne) was interested in the Ethical Culture movement—she even had a scholarship named after her at the Brooklyn Ethical Culture School. We were a family of readers and playgoers and though we lived in the Bedford section of Brookly, now an infamous Negro ghetto, it was

not then a predominantly Negro neighborhood. It did not become so, I believe, until the subway came past, some years after I was born....

Our house was four stories and narrow, as most brownstones are. The thing I always remember first about it was the iron fence that separated our yard from the sidewalk and from the houses on either side. What the white picket fence was to some parts of America, the iron fence was to Brooklyn in those days. Painted shiny black, each spike topped by a neat, arrow-shaped point, I suppose those fences were supposed to tell the world, This is Ours; we have arrived at the point where there is property that must, at least symbolically, be marked off and protected....

When I was born, my parents were living together in this house, but by the time I was old enough to have any memories of it they had split up and left me

there with my grand-parents.... How could a lovely, tender, indulged lady like my mother cope with a beautiful, young, wild, angry northern nonconformist like my father? As I observed them in later years, the only thing I could see they had in common was good looks....

That left four people at home—my grandparents, my Uncle Burke, and me. The others all offered me something. There was discipline from my grandmother, a little teasing and some jolly laughs with Uncle Burke before he ran out to join his friends in their activities, companionship on a grave and adult level from Grandad. And yet, we never meshed as a family unit. The house itself is the only thing that bound us all together, the only tangible I could touch that said "family" to me.

Looking back, I cannot remember my grandparents ever

exchanging more than a formal "Good morning, Mrs. Horne," "Good morning, Mr. Horne." Other than that they did not speak. If they needed to communicate Uncle Burke would carry notes from one to the other. I see their relationship, in memory, rather like a theatrical company, with my grandad as the producer, paying the bills, Uncle Burke as the stage manager, and my grandmother—no one else—as the director. Or to break that metaphor, the absolute dictator. She was a tiny woman, with very fair skin and gray-streaked hair. She wore rounded, steel-rimmed spectacles. She had a short, straight nose, a straight, rather thin mouth, and a very firm chin. . . .

I was nearly always with adults in Brooklyn. My association with children was limited to just a few in the neighborhood who met with Grandmother's approval. I was not allowed to play with the white children or with any children at all whose speech or deportment were not admirable in her eyes. When I was old enough to go to the Ethical Culture School (on my grandmother's scholarship) I was expected to leave school immediately at the end of the day and not see my classmates until the next morning. My grandmother did not believe in idle chitchat for herself or anyone else. Her conversation with me was always of an instructive nature: "Do as I say, do as I do! Don't cringe! Don't sulk! Stand straight! Speak clearly! Use your brains! Don't cry! Sit still in public! Be polite to those who are less fortu-

nate!" That was not to denote those with less money. In fact that didn't impress her at all. . . .

My grandmother's Sundays were usually spent in bed, sitting upright, reading, having a little tea and zwieback perhaps. It seemed as if she used the day to collect her strength for the coming week of activities. At suppertime Granddaddy would take me by the hand and we would walk down Chauncey Street to the delicatessen on Reid Avenue, where we would buy potato salad, cold cuts, baked beans, some kosher dills, anything we didn't have to cook. Then we would walk home, my grandfather nodding in his grave, dignified way to the neighbors, spread our feast on the kitchen table, and go! This was not just a Sunday event, but one that occurred several times a week as well.

On Sunday after dinner I was expected to report to my grandmother's room to say good night. I would say what I had been reading. I would be asked if I had clean clothes for the next day, told to stop biting my nails and then say my Catholic prayers. My grandmother practiced no religion herself but she believed any properly brought-up young lady should have religious training. Only when this had been accomplished to her satisfaction would I be dismissed to go to bed in the little room next to hers.

It was a strange life. I did not pay too much attention to the lack of communication between the adults in the house, because my Uncle Burke was the inter-

mediary and because of him I was not often very conscious of the strain between them.

As for my absent parents, I must say I missed them. My mother was never mentioned, but I had a tiny picture that I would look at and kiss. My father sent occasional letters and picture postcards and beautiful clothes and toys, and my grandmother would show me the postmarks, explaining this was the name of the place my father was now.

TWO FACES OF BROOKLYN. LEFT: SQUATTERS COLONY IN THE GOWANUS SECTION, 1934. TOP: ENJOYING THE STEEPLECHASE RIDE AT CONEY ISLAND.

Television producer

I don't have terribly fond memories of my

days in Brooklyn. Although there were people back then who

fueled my ambition for success, it was not in a very positive way.

One person was my older brother, Arthur. I had the misfortune

of being born on March 9, his birthdate too. When I was born

my family lived in a small walk-up apartment on Lincoln Place,

one block up from Eastern Parkway in Crown Heights. Arthur

was the perfect son, a boy who did extremely well in school,

excelled in sports, and was very much on the right side of so-

ciety. My parents adored him. From the moment I came along, I

MARTY

INGELS

lived in the shadow of perfect Arthur. Many of my early grade-school teachers gave me the same seat my brother had sat in, so I grew up with the driving ambition of trying to be just as good as Arthur. Probably the most telling example of how far his shadow extended was how my family celebrated our mutual birthday. Every year amid much fanfare, one birthday cake would be carried from the kitchen. In bold letters HAPPY BIRTHDAY ARTHUR was lettered across the top. Somewhere off the side of the cake *my* name was written. Not as bold, not even equal. Just hanging down off the side dripping in all that cake goo. The birthday cake symbolized my subordinate position.

Another influential person was my father. He was a very sweet, lovable man, who hid in his dresser drawers all kinds of funny masks and tricks that he'd bring to family parties to enter-tain the kids. He was a short, round man who was absolutely ill equipped to live in the rat race of Brooklyn. Every family in the neighborhood was striving to get ahead, but it seemed that no mat-ter how hard he tried, my father could never get over the top. He could never make things work. I hated the fact he couldn't cut it. My mother would bust his balls and ride his ass to do better, to go out and make something of himself. But it was to no avail. He owned an automotive brake shop on Jamaica Avenue that eventually went bankrupt. Not long after he suffered a series of heart attacks and from then on he was a different man. You could see life had beaten him. My uncles and aunts would come over to the apartment and they'd all put their heads together to see if they could think of a business for poor ol' Jack. But he could never get any of their ideas to work.

To carve out my own identity, I became the rebel in the family. I was the antithesis of perfect Arthur and I looked for ways to distance myself from my parents. I hung out with all the wrong guys and the wrong gangs. When the Italians moved into Crown Heights, I became one of them. I was the court jester in the Italian gangs that were running around the neighborhood, the funny Jew who would make all the crazy faces at the cops or throw water at people from the rooftops of the apartment buildings. I was the jokester and prankster, while Arthur continued to be perfect.

My gags extended beyond the street. At P.S. 167 on Eastern Parkway and Schenectady Avenue, I was the class clown. I would do anything for a laugh. I'd whistle at the teachers from the side of my mouth or blow cigarette smoke rings from underneath the desk. When I got to Erasmus Hall, my reputation preceded me. The teachers didn't take me for the serious student that Arthur was, and rightfully so. But I outfoxed them many times. I'd make up book reports in my English classes. I figured the teacher couldn't read every book in the world, so I'd get up in front of the class, create a title and author and ad-lib a book report.

The class knew it was total bullshit, but they loved every minute of it. I remember one particular report I concocted, a story about a Jewish family living in the South and how they coped with the anti-Semitism there. I went on and on, and shaded the story with all kinds of melodrama. At the end, the teacher praised me for an excellent report. She really put her foot in her mouth, though, when she mentioned how much *she'd* been moved after reading the book, too. The class fell apart. Till this day that teacher has no idea why everyone got so hysterical. I didn't know it back then, of course, but those times in Brooklyn were my start in show business.

Though my antics made me well known in school and on the streets, I was still living in the shadow of perfect Arthur. I was still the son of poor ol' Jack. Underneath all the gags, I felt like the loneliest guy in the world. And things grew worse. The only girlfriend I had was a girl who lived on President Street named Barbara Kaufman. I had a big crush on Barbara. I got to hang out with her because she was in the midst of recuperating from a broken leg and nobody would visit her.

For about four months, I'd go over to her house and we'd walk around the neighborhood. As soon as she got her cast off, she dumped me for another guy. And things got worse again. I was bar mitzvahed at the same time my father went broke. I remember celebrating my bar mitzvah in a small, crowded restaurant on Eastern Parkway,

when several years before, perfect Arthur had a big celebration at the Twin Cantors catering hall on Utica Avenue. I felt awful and cheated. That experience fueled my ambition that someday I'd beat perfect Arthur and be better than poor ol' Jack.

I brought my Brooklyn street humor out to Hollywood years later and quickly became a hit. I won a starring role in the successful *I'm Dickens, He's Fenster* television show and things were looking up. One day, after the first season, I telephoned my mother in Brooklyn, who told me things there weren't so good. My father was still having his attacks and he was constantly complaining about his decrepit car. I jumped on a plane and flew back to Brooklyn and decided to buy my father a new car. The gift was to be my crowning glory. The rebel, underachiever son was a star in Hollywood who wanted to share his success. I bought the car as soon as I landed in New York. I excitedly drove to Brooklyn and ran upstairs to the apartment and convinced him to take a ride with me. We got into the car and, after ten minutes, I handed him the keys. I told him the car was his. I wanted him to be proud of me. It was my moment of payback and I was finally at peace. But I wasn't allowed to relish that moment for too long. A week later my father passed away. He died in the car. So, for a troubled Jewish kid from Brooklyn, who suddenly found Hollywood success, I still couldn't rise above the pain of my past.

A N N E

It was 1933, the Depression held the

whole country in its grip, and New York was where the jobs were.

Daddy sold his barbershop in Tarentum, Pennsylvania, and pre-

ceded us to New York to find a home and a new job....

Anticipating the move to New York put us all in a fever of

excitement.... I pictured us riding around in big cars and living

in a penthouse overlooking the Statue of Liberty. Although I

couldn't quite visualize Mom sitting cross-legged, crooking her

little finger and swigging gin, I dreamed of all of us being

around "Manhattan babies," up 'til three, and tap-dancing on

J A C K S O N

42nd Street.

My dreams of city life were clearly fanciful, but nothing could have prepared us for the Old Mill Landing in Brooklyn, where Pop chose to settle. A contemporary account from *The Brooklyn Eagle* described the area in pleasantly neutral terms: "The individual with disdain for the comforts of civilization and eye for the picturesque can still get himself a house overlooking the melancholy reaches of Jamaica Bay for approximately $7.00 a month." The Old Mill Landing is not more than a mile away from the pushcarts, cinemas, and polylingual restaurants of Brownsville. From Crescent Street station on the elevated line a bus runs every 15 minutes." The Old Mill Landing was a minor resort abounding in swamps. A network of gray weathered boardwalks forked out from an old gristmill that gave

the area its name and led to damp summer cottages sitting up on wharf beams in the middle of Jamaica Bay. Pop saw them in summer at high tide with a moon dancing on the water, and he rented one for us.

We arrived at low tide, when the water had sunk back from the black mud, leaving a soggy marsh littered with orange peels and hideous green scum and stinking of decomposed vegetation. Mom hated it on sight.... "My God in heaven," she moaned, "he's gone and outdone himself with this rat hole." But I had inherited my father's eye for the picturesque and was delighted at living in a cottage by the sea. The idea of running along the railed wooden walks and seeing sea birds fly skyward over the tides into the September sunsets enraptured me. I grew pensive and romantic, dreaming of Dick Powell paddling me up a

lagoon as I trailed my hand through the cool water. The Old Mill's thousands of mosquitoes and gnats were excluded from my fantasy, but I fancied fireflies flickering in the distance as my lover wooed me on Jamaica Bay....

Not long after, Lil, our strange-looking neighbor in the kimono, came knocking on our door. Her hair was cut like Buster Brown's and she spoke with such a thick Brooklyn accent we thought she came from some exotic place. "Hell no," she said, contradicting my mother. "What, are ya kiddin'? I was born right heah in good ol' Brooklyn, up to Crescent Street."

She stood in our walkway at the open door. Mom was ashamed to invite her in because the "rat hole" was dank and "furnished in awful taste." Lil stood outside of everyone's doorway, though,

and even when invited in, she sedately refused. "No, I won't step in, I'm not dressed," she said, indicating her bathrobe and bedroom slippers. "There's gonna be a hurricane tonight, mussus. When the mister comes home, you better warn him and the kids. I gotta feelin' it be a whopper. Last one floated people's houses right away. We all had to 'vacuate and lie on our stomachs. Betta take your prayer books if you got 'em, 'cause you'll need His help with Her." "Her" was the hurricane.

Though we didn't evacuate, I remember that storm vividly. The rain cascaded on the roof. Daddy ran in from work soaked and breathless, eyeglasses in hand, his skin showing pink through his white shirt and trousers. The rain had plastered his hair to his head and the water sloshing in his shoes stained his white socks brown. I rushed to remove one shoe and my sister Beady the other as leftover raindrops gathered on his chin before dropping off his face. He seemed gleeful and exhilarated by the storm.

The lights flickered out, the radio went dead, lightning cut the sky, and thunder boomed, shaking our house. The gale winds stripped a shutter half off, leaving it flapping this way and that in the wind. The back door flew open and right off its hinges. My mother and even Beady were rigid with fear. Only Daddy and I seemed to enjoy the storm. "Oh, boy," he said, "that's some rain that we're having. Reminds me of 'Wreck of the Hesperus,' eh, Anna, so dammed good thing we not on boat." "We might as well be, John," Mom said angrily. "If we live through this awful night, I'm going to take the bus into City Line with you in the morning and find a decent place for us to live...." She would have her way; the storm marked the end of our stay in the home on stilts by the sea.

Singer

If I had been old enough, the seven tele-

phone lines in our Beekman Place apartment and my father's

proclivity for meeting weird-looking guys in Prospect Park

would have given me a clue what kind of business he was into.

But I was a young and sheltered Jewish girl from Flatbush, so I

hadn't the foggiest notion he was the neighborhood bookmaker.

In fact, I looked forward to our little walks in the park, where I

got the chance to meet my father's "business associates," fellows

like Curly, a guy who was as bald as a bat, or the other characters

he did business with. My personal favorite was a man my father

L A I N I E

K A Z A N

nicknamed Hangers. He was appropriately named because he walked like he had a wire clothes hanger stitched into his jacket. He was very pale and gaunt, and he had a perpetual shrug. I remember him as being one of my father's best customers, so we met with Hangers many times.

Other than these few charac-

FRIDAY NIGHT FOLK DANCES WERE A POPULAR ATTRACTION DURING THE EARLY 1900S IN MANY BROOKLYN SCHOOLS.

ters my father met in Prospect Park, the early years of my life were spent around family and close friends. My father came from a large family consisting of eight brothers and sisters, and my mother was one of nine children. Consequently there was family all over Brooklyn, so we saw relatives all the time.

Though I was never told so, I assumed the whole world was Jewish. Complementing the strong family values were the Judaic religious doctrines taught to me by my maternal grandmother. She would sit with me and read the Old Testament in her leisure hours. My grandmother possessed a very dynamic personality, a woman of strong character and inner strength. She had emigrated from Israel years before and, besides taking care of the household, she owned a grocery store in the area.

When I was about seven, a close playmate of mine invited me up to her apartment to see the Christmas tree in her family's living room. Her family had a farm in the country and they had just decorated their Christmas tree for the holidays. I had no idea what all this meant, but, spurred by her excitement, I eagerly wanted to see this tree. When I entered the room, I was captivated by the sight of a glittering, twinkling tree decorated with the colorful lights, silver garlands, and glistening Christmas ornaments. The beautiful Christmas figurines underneath the tree, depicting the birth of Christ, stood at solemn attention. It was a magical moment as I gazed at this Christmas tree, the soft glow of lights radiating throughout the cozy apartment in Brooklyn. After I returned home I asked my grandmother why we couldn't have a similar tree. When she explained the reasons, I suddenly realized there were other people in the world with different religions and faiths.

During my teenage years in Brooklyn, I did what all the other kids liked to do, which mainly consisted of one thing: hanging out at the local candy store. We spent hours on end hanging out at the candy store on the corner of Church and Flatbush Avenues, and the popular saying was "I'll see you at the Church." My father would get so angry at me for the time I spent at the candy store, he used to say, "You hang out there so much, I'm gonna move a bed there for you!" During the summer, the candy-store corner yielded to days at the Brighton Beach Baths. My other major interest was music. I loved to listen to the variety of music that was being played at the time, including the rhythm and blues sounds from Motown. My favorite, of course, was Frank Sinatra. Sinatra was one thing my parents and I agreed on. I remember how excited they would be when they got tickets for a Sinatra concert at the Paramount. While I got along well with my close-knit group of friends at the candy store, the large population of over six thousand kids at Erasmus Hall overwhelmed me. Oddly enough, during my senior year, I was voted the most popular girl of the 1960 graduating class.

One Brooklyn experience that wasn't much fun was the time I spent student teaching at James Madison High School. I was taking drama and speech education courses at Hofstra University on Long Island, commuting every day from my home in Brooklyn. Part of the requirement to obtain a degree was to teach in a high school. I was a child myself at the time, no more than twenty years old, and I was assigned to teach Madison seniors and juniors who were almost my age. It turned into a nightmare. Teaching this wild group of kids speech therapy during their lunch period was not my idea of an ideal teaching setting. They obviously didn't want to be there and I wasn't equipped to handle them. When I would ask them to sit in their seats, they would make lewd remarks about why they couldn't sit down. The wisecracks got worse as the class went on. I was horrified and at nights I would go home and cry. I ended up quitting the program after a couple of months.

When I first left Brooklyn and moved to California, there seemed to be something missing. It wasn't anything I could put my hands on, it was more like a feeling. I especially noticed it in the evening when I would turn in for the night. It finally dawned on me what it was. During my years at Beekman Place, we lived right over the BMT subway tracks and every few minutes a train would pass under my window. Most people who have lived near subways will tell you that over the years you get used to the noise. In a strange way, you count on it. After fifteen years of going to sleep with the subway as background noise, there was suddenly a void. It certainly is an odd memory. Yet hearing the clattering sounds of a subway when I walk in New York, brings back those wonderful, happy times of Flatbush in the fifties.

Comedian

I was known as the rotten kid of the family,

the neighborhood troublemaker, and the kid every daughter's

mother advised her to stay away from. And with good reason. I

was always getting into trouble with the school authorities or the

police, who would chase me off the street corners. Although I

had one natural sister, eight years my senior, I was raised in a

family with six other boys. They were cousins my mother took

into the house when their parents died. Getting into trouble and

clowning around was my way of standing out in the crowd. The

most important years of my life were spent in the Williamsburg

A L A N
K I N G

section of Brooklyn. They were the formative years, those late thirties and early forties, the years I crafted my act and met and fell in love with my wife. They were my early years in show business, when I performed at amateur shows at the RKO Republic, performances that eventually evolved into nightclub and television appearances.

They are years I can recall most vividly and times I look back on with great affection.

I was born on 295 South 2nd Street in Williamsburg. During the Depression, my family moved in with my grandfather because we had to give up our apartment. Times were tough. We lived in a five-story tenement fronted by a big stoop. Sigofsky's Grocery and a plumbing supply store were on the street level, standing like large bookends to the stoop. Mrs. Sigofsky was known as a wonderfully generous person in the neighborhood. She carried many families through the Depression, and God knows how she ever made a profit. She'd keep account of what everyone took

from the store, yet I rarely saw money exchange hands.

My grandfather was the superintendent of the building. He also served as an itinerant rabbi and frowned on my unruliness, which stemmed from my father. My father was raised under the tenets of a strict Orthodox Jewish family in Poland, and, when he came to America, he immediately rebelled. He was a guy who was looked at by everyone in the neighborhood as a little off the wall. He was the oddball of the family, the misfit who possessed a great intellect. While everyone was looking out for his family, my father was busy lobbying for socialist and unionist causes. He was the epitome of an iconoclast. Whatever everyone was for, my father was against. My parents were a great match. My mother was a daughter of a rabbi. My father was an atheist. As odd as he was, he was an extremely stimulating man who encouraged me to think and explore. He turned out to be the most influential person in my life.

Until I got rich, I never realized we were so poor. There was always food on the table, and it wasn't drummed into us how bad we had it. Television wasn't glamorizing the rich-and-famous lifestyle. My first big break in show business came in junior high school. It was the day my music teacher, Mrs. Berkfeld, looked the other way so I could take the school's drum set home to play a gig. I had formed a dance band called Earl Knight and the Musical Knights. Along with four other broken-down kids from

Williamsburg I'd go into the cellar clubs in the neighborhood and play a few songs. After each performance we'd pass the hat. Cellar clubs were popular back then. They were converted basements in brownstone buildings. We played a lot of cellar clubs on Bedford Avenue as well as other places in Flatbush. Besides playing the drums, I also fronted the band by doing comedy routines and impressions. I had an amazing memory for dialogue and comedy. My father was the only one in the family who knew I was playing these gigs. He supported my comedic and musical ambitions and recognized I wasn't a student. He was right: the best memory I have of grammar school was playing penny craps in the P.S. 19 schoolyard.

I supplemented the tips I made from my musical combo with jobs I worked during the day. I had a million jobs growing up. My first job was delivering milk in brown paper bags to tenement apartments. After I worked in a barber shop sweeping the floors, I got a job racking pool balls at Joe Reds' poolroom on Roebling Street. For a while I boxed suits in a haberdashery called Dobson's. The best job I had was in a luncheonette called the Hicks Shop. I was a soda jerk and sandwich maker. It was across the street from Eastern District High School, making it a great place to hold court. There were lots of people who came in there, and I'd tell jokes, do impressions, and sing. I was fine-tuning my act behind the counter. My wife, whom I knew from Williamsburg since I was

ten, was attending Eastern District High School at the same time I was popular in the Hicks Shop. She'd come in to the luncheonette to visit me.

I also polished my craft by entering all the amateur shows in Brooklyn. I'd really get a rise out of the audiences singing "Brother, Can You Spare a Dime." I'd sing the song wearing knickers and a pea cap that newspaper boys wore at the time. The crowd loved my rendition. I always enjoyed singing. I was a singing usher in a local theater in Flatbush where I would lead the audience in song. They took their cue by following the bouncing ball above the lyrics on the screen.

My parents, while always struggling, never lost their sense of humor. They loved to tease each other. My father held a slew of jobs. We had a sewing machine in the house, and he'd do cuffs for the neighbors. Or he'd make and sell leather belts. He once worked for the Socialist Party, though he made very little money from that. On weekends he'd sell Hooverettes, which were house dresses named after another brain surgeon we elected into the White House. While my father was a stimulating man intellectually, financially he was a failure. Because he came from Warsaw, my mother use to quip he was the first Polish joke that came to America. My mother spent most of her time in the kitchen. In fact, that room was the center of the household. The pots and pans were always going. We had a big oak table in the middle of the kitchen that every-

one sat around, and she loved to cook. The problem was my mother was a lousy cook. She never believed the butcher had killed the meat. She'd cook things to death for days. I can still smell a brisket or *schmalz* cooking three blocks away. That always takes me back to my days in Brooklyn. In those rare instances when my mother cooked something that actually tasted good, my father would turn to her with a straight face and say, "Minnie, you made a mistake. This meal tastes really good!"

Growing up in Williamsburg was like living in a small town. Everyone knew each other. The kids were full of energy and the streets were always full of activity. The adults were a different story. They all looked very, very old. Some of my relatives who, as I look back, were only fifty years old, looked ancient. It was as if they had given up on their own lives and were living their future through their children. While we were out playing in the street having a great time, they were buying week-old bread with relief stamps from Dugan's bakery. My parents sacrificed everything they had for us.

When I dropped out of Boys High School, my mother was devastated. She couldn't see a future for me without a formal education. My father, meanwhile, continued to support my act. He believed in me. He saw I was happy doing my thing, and I could do nothing wrong in his eyes. My greatest personal satisfaction is that they both got to see my success later on.

CNN television and radio
talk show host

OVERLEAF: THE RKO
ALBEE ON FULTON STREET
WAS A POPULAR MOVIE
THEATER IN BROOKLYN.

For years, whenever I saw a police squad

car I got a sick feeling in the pit of my stomach. Saturday morning, June 10, 1944, I was carrying home a load of books from the library when I saw them: three squad cars parked in front of the apartment building. Instinctively I ran to the front door and up the stairs to our third-floor walk-up. Before I got to the door, I heard my mother screaming. I was ten years old and terrified. On the landing I ran into one of the police officers, who scooped me up and carried me back downstairs and put me into the flivver. (Squad cars were called "flivvers" in my neighborhood.)

L A R R Y

K I N G

We started to drive, and slowly, and with much compassion, he told me that my father had died of a heart attack. The two of us drove around most of the day. He told me I was the man of the house now and that my mother needed me to be brave. Not wanting to leave me, the cop took me to the matinee at the Loews Pitkin: *Bataan*, with Robert Taylor. (I interviewed Taylor twenty-five years later and he was touched when I told him of the incident.)

That summer we moved from our third-floor walk-up to the Bensonhurst section of Brooklyn—to an attic apartment across the street from my mother's sister, my Aunt Bessie. When school started that fall, I had to begin all over again: new friends, new teachers, new surroundings. Larry, the whiz kid, never did well in school again; the things that had seemed important once just weren't important anymore. . . .

I went to Lafayette High, and the kids who graduated from there during my era are incredible: there are surgeons, judges, businessmen. Herb Cohen was a classmate, as was Mutual president Marty Rubinstein. Sandy Koufax graduated from the same school one year later. . . .

In many ways the neighborhood was as important an influence on my own life as was my immediate family. Bensonhurst was like a small village—it was *Fiddler on the Roof* transposed to America. The two major ethnic groups populating this corner of Brooklyn were Italians and Jews. These two groups share many characteristics: they are warm, family-oriented, hardworking, and loud. On any afternoon near suppertime, windows started opening and you could hear a chorus of mothers yelling: "Tony!" "Vito!" "Myron!" "Seymour!" I was sure the whole world was Jewish and Italian, and I believed Italian was a religion as well as a country of origin. I suppose I knew from the movies that there were "regular" Americans—WASPs, as we now call them—but they lived in strange places like Ohio and Kansas.

What helped keep the neighborhood so self-contained was that it was unnecessary to leave it for any earthly need. There was the grocery store, Langer's with its pickle barrel that we regularly dipped into. The bakery, Ebinger's, with its charlotte russes; the movie theater; the candy store . . . the essential one was without doubt the candy store. The candy store was a place to get candy; it had jars of those wonderful one-cent tooth-destroying sweets. But it was much more than that. It had a soda fountain—egg creams were considered the elixir of life—a few tables, newspapers and magazines, and a jukebox. For most of my childhood, the candy store was run by a man named Sam Maltz who had a hate-hate relationship with the kids in the neighborhood. He referred to us all as bandits, which he pronounced "ban-deets." Since none of us ever had much money, Sam was always trying to throw us out of the store for loitering. . . .

Compared with kids of today, we were, to say the least, unsophisticated, and our sources of information on the outside world were limited. For us, the movies provided the most powerful view of the world. Americans were like Gary Cooper, and Americans were brave, true, strong, and good. Period. Every Saturday we went to the Benson Theater and had this knowledge reaffirmed. Because so many of the movies of that era were about the war, and because we wanted to emulate our heroes in whatever way we could, we conducted major battles right there in the Benson. In spite of the greatness of so many of the movies of the forties, Hollywood had a terrible habit of putting love scenes or musical numbers into these movies. Our sensibilities were righteously offended by this muck, and during these celluloid interludes we heaved "ammo"—Jujubes and Goobers were favorites—at our enemies of the week. . . .

When we weren't at the movies, or in the candy store, or playing ball, we were on the stoop. The stoop was a social mecca—at least during our early years. When we became more mature, we graduated to the corner. On the stoop we sat and talked, made up games, argued about sports. Part of my skill as a broadcaster was honed on the stoop. During lulls in conversation—I've never been able to stand dead air—I announced passing cars or pedestrians. I also reconstructed, play by play, sporting events I'd gone to that

the other guys might not have seen. I did the same with movies. It usually took me two hours and a half to tell the story of a ninety-minute film.

Even as a kid I was fascinated with radio, and wanted to be on it. I constantly fantasized about being an announcer—to be an announcer, I was sure, was to achieve the ultimate position in life. I wondered all about an-nouncers: were they as tall and distinguished as they sounded? Did they stand or sit? Where did they get breaking sports and news from? I used to walk down the street announcing to myself, oblivious as to how weird I must have looked....

When I first moved to Ben-sonhurst, before I got to know anybody, the radio was my only friend. It was the first thing I saw in the morning, and the last thing I heard at night. Part of its impact came from its sheer phys-ical presence. It was large, of polished dark wood, and shaped like a temple. In his book *Work-ing*, Studs Terkel points out that very few people end up doing what they would like to do for their livelihood. I am one of the lucky ones in that respect. I got inside the temple.

As a youngster I was a bicycle messenger

for the Civil Defense Department, which coordinated the air

raid drills during World War II. I looked forward to those drills

when the siren blared, causing people to scurry hither and

Actor

thither. When the alarming commotion faded into tranquillity, I

OVERLEAF: CIVIL DEFENSE DEPARTMENT VOLUNTEERS PREPARE FOR AN AIR RAID DRILL DURING WORLD WAR II.

had sole run of the neighborhood. Proudly wearing my Civil

Defense helmet, emblazoned with the bright CD sticker, I rode

my bicycle from shelter to shelter delivering messages to and

from air raid wardens. It was exciting pedaling through the

suddenly dark and empty streets of Brooklyn, and especially

MARTIN LANDAU

133

enchanting were moonless nights when the streets were absolutely pitch black. Not a soul could be seen, and cars were parked askew, abandoned by their occupants, who had sought refuge in a nearby shelter or basement. As I cycled through Flatbush, the absolute stillness and calming serenity of those streets created a perverse excitement. The pure silence was in sharp contrast to the irreverent noise and wild vitality that was the usual scenario.

I lived with two older sisters and my parents at 3335 Bedford Avenue, just a couple of steps away from Avenue L. The war was just one of many distractions for me during my days in Brooklyn. Our household was always full of energy and noise, especially alive with a great deal of talking. Because I was a naturally quiet child, I was in awe of the bustling activity that took place in my house. But I would usually escape into my own world by reading the comic strips that appeared in the Sunday papers. I was very intrigued by these fictional characters, the world of Maggie and Jiggs and Andy Gump, lives that could be created simply by putting pen to paper. I'd look at these comics in the Sunday *Journal*, the *Mirror*, and the *Daily News* and make up my own dialogue. I became so fascinated and charmed with these comic strips that when I grew older I began to cartoon. While attending James Madison High School, I became the sports cartoonist for the *Madisonian* and I landed a job with the *New York Daily News* as a staff artist

on the Andy Gump strip.

Though I got along well with my peers, I was something of an individualist growing up. I realized early on I was not one who embraced structured group activity. I felt uncomfortable at my first and only Cub Scout meeting at P.S. 193. The militaristic slant of the troop meeting gave me an uneasy feeling. Unlike most boys there, I didn't like the fact I had to wear a uniform, stand in line, and do the same activities everyone else was doing. I left, never to return. Similarly, when I became bored or disenchanted with my teachers in school, or didn't like the way a teacher treated the students, I took it upon myself to go home. My poor mother was horrified at this habit. Two teachers gradually cured me of this practice, though for totally different reasons. The first teacher was Mrs. Roach, a wonderful teacher who inspired her students, a woman who was very caring and extremely sensitive to the learning process. I enjoyed Mrs. Roach's class and remember her lessons well. The second teacher was Miss Fishman. Miss Fishman was an exceptionally attractive woman, possessing the most incredible body I'd ever seen. I remember looking at her a lot. Unlike the noble feelings I had for Mrs. Roach, my urges toward Miss Fishman were more carnal in nature. Miss Fishman initiated my first adolescent stirrings of seeing women in that light. As a twelve-year-old, this was the beginning of a very exciting discovery. The habit of leaving school in the middle of the day was forevermore

remedied.

My circle of friends enjoyed going to the movies or playing in the streets. Vacation days were spent watching Jimmy Cagney in *The Fighting 69th* or Charles Laughton in *The Hunchback of Notre Dame*. The magical novelty of the cool and crisp air-conditioned air in the Avalon or the Elm was always a treat on a hot summer day. We also spent many hours playing with our yo-yos or arcos. I was especially adept with the arco. Shaped like an hourglass on its side, an arco was thrown and caught by a string. I could throw an arco higher than any building in the neighborhood, or keep it spinning on the string. I was one of the most proficient kids in the neighborhood with that toy. Another game I liked was territory with knives, a game played on a flat, dirt patch. After dividing a four-by-two-foot patch in half, two opponents threw knives into each other's territory, wiping away the previous borderlines. The game would at first go very quickly, but as it progressed it became more finite. Whoever captured the most territory first was declared the winner.

Flatbush had a wonderful network of alleyways squeezed between the neighborhood's parking garages, through which you could make your way to many parts of the neighborhood. I belonged to a Bedford Avenue group called the Dragons, which was always at odds with the group of kids from East 28th Street. When we got into a scuffle, we'd eventually use this maze to get back to safer turf. I could work my way back to Bedford and Avenue L using these routes. Only through many hours in the street could a kid fully learn all the possibilities of traveling through that complex web of alleyways. One time, though, I wasn't so fortunate. One evening my mother sent me out on an errand, and I ran up against the East 28th gang, who were angry at my group of friends. They dragged me into one of the backyards and tied and gagged me to a clothesline pole and left me shivering in the winter night. When I didn't return home, my mother called the police. Several hours later, when I saw a policeman's flashlight come swinging down the alleyway, I was finally rescued. The Dragons naturally got even several months later.

When he was twelve, my father emigrated from Austria to New York, where he met my "Yankee" mother. She was from a German-Jewish family that had come to America several generations before. A "Yankee" was someone who had roots in America, and my father kiddingly used the term when he referred to my mother. He was a warm family man as well as a great storyteller. I used to cherish the times my father would tell me the story of how he and his singing group got pelted with rotten produce as they sang on the Bushwick Theater stage during an amateur show. He had such a good time telling that story. He would laugh hysterically as he described the moment when, just as the tenor began to harmonize (my father was the baritone), out

from the darkness came the fruits and vegetables. He kiddingly blamed the poor tenor for not making it in show business. He would tell that story over and over for years, and there was something very special in his laugh as he recounted the tale.

Because he wanted to quickly assimilate into the American life-style, my father only spoke English around the house. I was forever astonished, therefore, by the number of languages I gradually learned he knew. Many an afternoon we would walk along Bedford Avenue and meet some of his immigrant

friends along the way. He would commiserate with each of them, shifting easily into Polish, Russian, Hebrew, or German, as each situation demanded. As I got older I would study these people as well as all the other people I saw riding on the subways. What type of accent is that? What does he do for a living? Where did they come from? Where are they going? I developed an interest in the lives of people while I studied and analyzed their mannerisms. Those exercises proved to be a great foundation for what I do today.

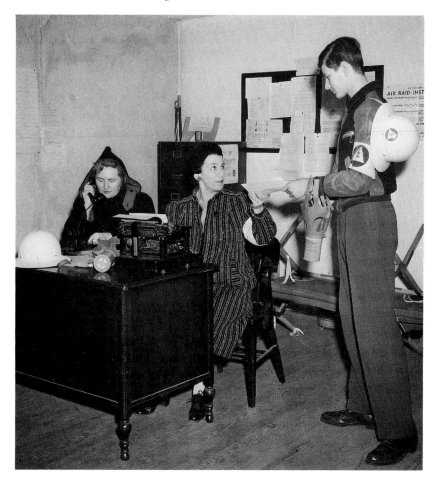

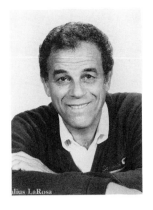
Julius LaRosa

Singer

I've been singing for as long as I can re-

member. As a young boy I enjoyed the popular standards of the

day, tunes made famous by Frank Sinatra, Bing Crosby, and Dick

Haymes. During my early years I never had any ambition to

become a professional singer, and I never dreamed that one day I

would sing for a living. My fondness for singing certainly wasn't

inherited. My father was the only person who could be remotely

described as a singer in the family and that was after he indulged

in a couple of glasses of homemade wine. We lived in a tiny four-

room railroad apartment that consisted of a kitchen, two bed-

JULIUS
LAROSA

rooms, and a living room. Although I enjoyed carrying a tune, I was very bashful as a child, so I would go into my bedroom, close the French doors, and sing there. My parents and my older sister would usually be in the kitchen or living room. They enjoyed my singing but didn't dare open the bedroom doors. I first soloed in front of an audience while singing in the chorus at Grover Cleveland High School. After I finished and heard the applause, I realized audiences weren't so bad after all.

My parents emigrated from Palermo, Sicily, arriving in Brooklyn during the years when masses of Italians came to this country for a better opportunity and higher-paying jobs. When I was first born, we lived on Irving Avenue, but we soon moved to Jefferson Avenue, which skirted the Bushwick-Ridgewood border of Brooklyn and Queens. I enjoyed a comfortable family environment. While my mother took care of the home, my father tended to his radio repair business. He owned and operated several stores in Brooklyn, though not at the same time. We'd tease him that he was a tycoon of a chain of stores. The only problem was that when he opened a new store, he'd close another at the same time. Nevertheless, though the family wasn't rich, there never was a need that went unfulfilled. While most of the family's activities took place in Brooklyn, the big event in the summer was traveling to Babylon, Long Island, to go clamming. My father would wake us at five o'clock on a Saturday morning and we'd begin our journey to Babylon. In those days, traveling on Sunrise Highway to the reaches of Long Island from Brooklyn was like driving across the country. It was an eighty-mile trip that took forever. After arriving home that same evening, we'd divvy up our clam catch and recuperate on the front stoop from our journey. We'd spend the evening listening to the conversations of the old ladies who leaned from their pillow-cushioned windowsills.

The family environment was warm and caring, and while my parents enjoyed a good relationship with each other, there were times when they didn't see eye to eye. One such argument was over a rent increase. Apparently the monthly rent bill was raised five dollars because the Jefferson Avenue landlord converted to steam heat from oil. My parents quibbled for days whether to accept the increase or move out. We eventually stayed, but that five dollars in additional rent precipitated a lively discussion. My sister and I assumed the argument hadn't been too bad, however, because my father still wore his mustache. Usually, after a particularly stormy round with my mother, my father would shave off his mustache. He developed this amusing habit many years before. She obviously liked him with facial hair, but he'd childishly spite her by shaving it off. The mustache eventually became a barometer for the mood of the house. If my sister and I arrived home and saw my father sporting a nonmustached face around the apartment, we knew trouble was in the air and it was best for us to stay out of sight.

During the late 1930s I was at an age when I began to explore the neighborhood with my friends. On many summer nights we'd cross over into Queens and occasionally stumble onto a

storefront in Ridgewood, which was primarily a German neighborhood. Prominently displayed in the windows were flags with swastikas. Filtering out from the doorway were rousing shouts of *"Sieg Heil! Sieg Heil!"* Other times we'd wander by an open social garden or the doorway of a decorated ballroom holding similar gatherings. As youngsters, we never gave these so-called Bund meetings much thought. Only after America got involved in the war and these meetings ceased, was it explained to us what they were. By this time, the threat of a German offshore submarine attack on Brooklyn was imminent, and everyone was preparing accordingly. One defensive strategy that was used to protect the neighborhood from an attack was painting the upper half of an automobile's headlight. By using black paint, the headlight's glare couldn't be seen from the ocean. This would hamper the submarines from zeroing in on cars, Civil Defense officials explained.

Although I was an average student at P.S. 123, I had a propensity for asking an older friend the correct meaning of newfound words. I was fascinated with new words and wanted to know their meaning with the eventual purpose of incorporating them into my vocabulary. There was something ironic in my doing that, because I wasn't an avid reader. Somewhere along the way, I developed a fascination with the meanings of words, which later in life fueled my rabid interest to read. I finally overcame my shyness and

began the formal aspect of my singing career in high school. I joined the chorus at Grover Cleveland and eventually was selected to the All-City chorus under the direction of Peter J. Wilhousky. The more cheers I heard after I soloed, the more I began to regard singing as a career.

The most loving person in the LaRosa family was my father's sister, Aunt Rosie. The whole family lived within a four-block radius in Bushwick, so there was close contact with the relatives. Although there were several other aunts and uncles, the kids in the family were especially drawn to Aunt Rosie. She was everybody's favorite aunt. A remarkably warm, loving young woman, Aunt Rosie had the wonderful capacity to make each one of her nieces and nephews feel special. She would take your hand and caress your cheek and make you feel you were the best. For years we'd argue who was her favorite niece or nephew. We do it, kiddingly, today. When Aunt Rosie got married in 1943, left Brooklyn, and went off to Illinois to live with her husband, there was a terrible sense of emptiness among the children. But thankfully the LaRosa family is still blessed with Aunt Rosie's presence. She was a loving young woman then, and she is a loving older woman today. She touched and changed our lives with an affection that will always be remembered.

I was born Barry Alan Pincus, the son of

Harold Killiher, a thin Irishman who drove a truck for the

Schaefer brewery. I don't know anything else about him because

Singer

my parents were divorced when I was a baby. All he gave me was

his mother's maiden name, Pincus. I was raised by my mother,

Edna, and my grandparents, Esther and Joseph Manilow. They

wouldn't allow my father to visit, and the few times his name was

mentioned it was always with loathing. I grew up thinking I'd

better stay away from the guy. But I grew up loving my grand-

mother, although the rest of the family feared her; adoring my

B A R R Y
M A N I L O W

grandfather, although the rest of the family derided him; and worshiping my mother, although the family never understood her.

My grandparents were immigrants from Russia, who, along with hundreds of other immigrants, wound up living in a tenement apartment in Williamsburg, Brooklyn, New York. The apartment was in an enormous building near the elevated BMT subway and a few blocks away from the Williamsburg Bridge and the East River. The apartments they lived in were small and cold. There was hardly any furniture; they could afford barely enough food to sustain them. . . .

Gramma married Grampa not out of love, but because her

father demanded it. She eventually wound up loving him (how could she not?), but she was always frustrated at her lot in life. . . .

Other than my immediate family, the two most important people in my young life were Larry and Fred.

Larry Rosenfeld was my first friend. He was five-eight—I'll never forget it because he always felt he was too short. He had jet-black hair and a perfect nose (everyone had a perfect nose compared to mine). . . . Larry introduced me to Fred Katz, my second real friend. He lived across the street with his father, younger sister, and brother. His mother had died of cancer the year before—he could have gone

in a million directions. . . .

The three of us had that kind of wonderful inseparable friendship you can only have when you're growing up. My apartment became our base of operations. After school the three of us would burst into Gramma's kitchen, gulp down the milk and cookies she'd have waiting for us, and tear out into the street. We'd race down Division Avenue, past the police station, past Kitzel Park where all the old Jews sat, until we got to the schoolyard, where we'd meet the rest of the gang and roller skate on the newly paved street in front of the school.

Larry, Fred, and I teamed up with the usual cast of school characters. We began going to after-school parties where the girls taught the boys to dance as *American Bandstand* played on television. We'd all rush home from school to watch the show at three o'clock and got very involved in the lives of Bob, Justine, and the other regulars on the show. We learned how to stroll and lindy and philly. . . .

I found a steady girl. Her name was Maxine Horn. She was a sweet girl. Tall and skinny like me, with a great sense of humor. Her family was bright; her brothers and sisters were all college graduates, something very rare in Williamsburg. Once when I got home from dropping Maxine off after a school dance, I called Fred and excitedly told him that when I kissed her good night, her leg went up in the back, just like in the movies. I think my friendship with these two funny, intelligent, gentle souls was the reason I was able to get through an uncomfortable adolescence.

One afternoon, while I was on my way home from Larry's apartment, a Schaefer beer delivery truck pulled alongside me. A tall, skinny guy jumped out of the driver's side and walked over to me. "Hi, Barry," he said.

"Hi," I said. He looked familiar.

"I'm your father," he said. And I instantly knew he was.

Whenever anyone had ever mentioned Harold's name, Gramma would grumble disgustedly and Mom would get angry. There was only one picture of him in all our photo albums. Gramma had quietly taken the scissors and cut him out of any photos he was in with Edna and me. But I recognized him from that one stray photo.

"How've you been, son?" he asked.

"Okay," I said looking at the ground, feeling awkward.

"Listen, I know your grandma hates me and I'm afraid if she sees me she'll call the cops, so I'm not gonna stay long, but tomorrow's your birthday and I brought you a present." He reached into the cab of the truck and lifted out a reel-to-reel tape recorder. "Here," he said, handing it to me. "It's not brand-new, but I thought you'd get a kick out of playing with it."

"Thanks!" I said. "This is great!"

"You got a kiss for your old man?" he asked.

I hugged him tentatively and kissed him on the cheek. We let go and he looked at me for a long

minute.

"Okay. I've gotta go. You take care of yourself. Hey, how's your mother?"

"She's fine," I said.

"Listen, don't tell anyone I was here, huh? Tell 'em you found the tape recorder or something, okay?" He walked briskly to the driver's side of the truck. "Be a good kid," he said and waved and drove off in the giant beer truck.

I stood there with my new tape recorder, bursting with excitement, but feeling funny, too. For as long as I could remember, I had thought of Harold as this monster person who had been mean to Mom and was uncaring and ugly. Now, here was this nice-looking, gentle guy, treating me affectionately, remembering my birthday, and giving me a great gift. That was my father? He wasn't so bad after all. I brought the tape recorder into the apartment.

"Where'd you get that?" Gramma immediately asked.

"Where'd I get what?" I said, stalling.

"Where'd you get that machine?" she said.

"What machine?" I said, still stalling, trying to think of where I could possibly have gotten it.

"*This* machine, in your hands, where did you get it?" she said, losing her patience.

"Oh, *this* machine," I said, finally acknowledging the tape recorder.

"Yes, darling, that one. Where did you get it?"

I'm a terrible liar. Always have been. I just couldn't lie to

her. "Well," I said, taking a deep breath, "the funniest thing happened just now, Gramma. Harold drove by in his truck and gave it to me for my birthday," I stuttered out. "Are you gonna hit me?"

"*Harold?*" she yelled. "That *monster!* Where is he?" She ran out into the street.

I ran after her. "Gramma! Gramma! He's gone. Come back!"

She ran up the street looking for Harold, the monster, while I got some milk and cookies. When she came back, she was muttering to herself and I was in my room, glowing over my new tape recorder. "If I didn't see you loving this thing so much," she said, "I'd throw it out in the garbage."

I was very quiet. I was hoping she'd just forget about it.

When Mom came home and heard about my visitor, she was upset, too. It was a topic of conversation for a few days and then the subject was dropped. Soon we all began to enjoy the new tape recorder because Mom sang a song into it and suddenly the machine wasn't so bad after all.

I never felt the need to go searching for my father, and so I never did. I got so much love and I felt so secure with my family and my friends that finding my real father never became an issue. Besides, the family would have gotten really upset, and I was never one to make waves. But the image of that gentle man, Harold the Monster, who hugged me and gave me my first tape recorder for my eleventh birthday, stayed with me.

Film director

One of the most vivid memories I have of

Brownsville during the 1930s was how alive its streets were. There always seemed to be people out in the street: on the stoops, in doorways, on fire escapes—there were people everywhere. It was a neighborhood where people, when learning Pearl Harbor had been bombed, ran out in the street and yelled to each other, "The Japs bombed Pearl Harbor!" "The Japs bombed Pearl Harbor!" Or when Roosevelt died, they quietly walked along the sidewalk or sat weeping on their stoops. Brownsville wasn't a place where people sat inside their apart-

PAUL
MAZURSKY

ments and insulated themselves from their neighbors. They were people who lived, laughed, cried, and struggled together. The flavor of the neighborhood was best exemplified by our next-door neighbor. She made it her business to know everyone else's business. She was constantly leaning out her window, watching the world go by, and when you arrived home she was able to tell you exactly everything that happened in your apartment house that day. When I filmed *Next Stop, Greenwich Village* many years later, I wrote a character into the movie inspired by that woman.

I lived on Bergen Street and spent a lot of my time in my grandfather's candy store around the corner on Saratoga Avenue. The store was the big neighborhood hangout for the kids as well as for the older men. The old-timers would come in and buy the *New York Daily News* or the Yiddish paper *The Forward*, and kibitz with my grandfather in the store. While they kept themselves busy talking, smoking, and arguing politics, the kids ordered two-cent egg creams. It was like one big family gathering. The character of the store was exactly what you'd find in the delicatessen, the butcher shop, the cleaners, and the grocery next door. Because the stores were owned by someone who lived in the neighborhood, when people stopped in, it would turn into a grand social event.

My grandfather was a very special man. When I look back on the time I spent with him, I realize how fortunate I was to

have been his grandson. He was a little Jewish guy from Russia who walked with a bad leg. But his most impressive feature was his very active mind. When he came to America, his immediate ambition was to teach himself to read English. His goal was to re-read in English all the books he had read in Russian. I remember the long hours he'd spend reading Dostoyevski, Tolstoy, Turgenev, and Pushkin. He was a guy who started out rolling cigars for a living and then one day bought his own candy store business in Brownsville. And in his spare time—when he had the time—he would satisfy his passion by reading the great Russian authors. When I wasn't hanging out with him in the candy store, I'd visit with him in his apartment. While my grandmother was busy serving me a glass of tea—which I'd immediately pour into a saucer and sip, all the while sucking on a piece of sugar—my grandfather would tell me stories about old Russia, including great tales of Peter the Great and Ivan the Terrible.

I was born into the typical Brownsville family: we were very poor. My father couldn't find work in the thirties until the WPA began. While he worked as a laborer, my mother helped out by getting a job playing piano for a children's dancing school. She also worked as a typist. Although conditions in Brownsville were very rough, there was very little neighborhood crime. Stealing from each other was out of the question, so you didn't need to lock your apartment door or

worry about your neighbors. Outside of the gang fights between the blacks and the whites, or fights between ethnic gangs, you never heard about a woman getting raped or people getting mugged and murdered for a few pennies. Drugs weren't part of the scene either. If anything, people looked to help each other. I remember a kid in the neighborhood whose father was very nice to everybody in the building. Every year during Passover he would give a big bag of food to about ten families in the building. The guy, I later found out, turned out to be a gangster who probably worked for Murder Inc. But the streets were safe because people cared for each other and the gangsters watched the neighborhood. It was safer living in 1930s Brownsville with the guys from Murder Inc. than it is living in Beverly Hills today. Such was the irony of those days.

I was known as a funny kid in the neighborhood, a kid who made the other guys laugh. I was also very good playing street games, although my mother was always screaming for me to come in and do my homework. From P.S. 44 grammar school, I went to Junior High School 178, then to Thomas Jefferson High School, and finally to Brooklyn College. By merely taking a bus, I went from one neighborhood school to another, from grammar school to college. I was bitten by the acting bug in junior high school when I landed my first role in a school play about Thomas Edison. I was ten years old and knew immediately that acting was what I wanted to do.

When I graduated, a favorite teacher, Philip Gross, wrote in my autograph book, "An actor you shall be!"

Although everyone was struggling to get ahead, it wasn't a bottom-line world. Possessions didn't carry great weight. The richest kid on Bergen Street was a guy named Bobby Goldstein.

He was considered rich because his father had a car. But money didn't matter because, for the most part, everything was cheap. Or you'd find ways to save money. We'd sneak into the movies by walking in backward. Or chip in and pay for one ticket and the guy inside would open the side door. I loved going to the

movies with my friends. My mother would make me her specialty sandwich that included halvah and banana on challah. I'd sit in the dark, watch the movie, and munch away. It was a great way to spend a Saturday afternoon.

WPA PROJECTS IN THE MID 1930s HELPED RENOVATE AND BUILD BROOKLYN'S STREETS AND TROLLEY LINES.

Opera singer

My mother was a woman of ferocious de-

termination to make herself into an opera singer. But, as Olivier

said, it's the gift and the skill that make for success, and she

never had the opportunity to develop the skill. She was the

daughter of a Warsaw tailor, the only man in the family not a

cantor.... A wealthy Pole had heard her soprano voice and of-

fered to subsidize her training for opera. Since relations be-

tween Jewish tailors and Polish aristocrats were not at the time

well integrated, her family rejected the offer. She never forgave

her parents or my father, also a tailor, for not having the money

ROBERT MERRILL

to make her an opera star. And she never let me forget it, either.

I made my unpromising debut in this world, yowling and kicking, on the kitchen table of a sixth-floor cold-water flat on South 2nd Street, Williamsburg. It could only have been a very conventional scream, but somehow it persuaded my mother that I was a singer, and from that moment my life was laid out for me. I would be her replacement.

What I wanted to do was play baseball. And she persistently blocked the baselines. As soon as I learned to walk, she decided I had a weak heart, a "leaky valve," and I would have to walk slowly, breathe deeply, and not "run around in the sun like a crazy dog." When I wanted to sell newspapers to make money for a ball and glove, she said, "No, that's how gangsters start." I did not realize she was preserving my hands for piano lessons. I had to wear heavy gloves in fall and winter, and the slightest scratch on my fingers brought out an armor-plate of gauze wrapping, Vaseline, and bandages torn from tattered sheets.

I managed to see the Dodgers play, but that was my father's secret. Boy Scouts were admitted free to Ebbets Field once a week. Though my father now operated a sewing machine in a factory, his tailor's fingers had not lost their skill. He found a fabric that matched the Scouts', all the way down to the long green stockings. The Dodgers were giants in those days—Dazzy Vance, Babe Herman, Hack Wilson—and I even saw Babe Ruth clout two homers at Yankee Stadium by courtesy of the Scouts.

I was in demand on our block when the sides were chosen—and an empty lot was available. I had a knuckler and a floater that went up like a balloon and looked so easy that they wrenched their backs reaching for it.

The block was my whole world. It demanded, and I gave, complete loyalty....

Our block stank in summer and froze in winter, and many of my friends died of the flu or pneumonia. We were always short of money, but we never thought of ourselves as underprivileged or hopeless. Since I never ventured far from our block, I assumed this was the way everybody lived. All of us had to pal around with each other. If you strayed into one of those Irish or Italian blocks, who was going to help you?

But my security here was undermined by Mamma's goddamn Caruso records. Bing Crosby and Russ Columbo were what we listened to on the radio and whistled on the street. "Let's Fall in Love," "It's Only a Paper Moon." Caruso was "long-hair stuff" and suspiciously sissy. Merely listening to opera music could brand you a fruit. And then whom would you have to hang around with? Your sister.

My mother worshiped Caruso's voice. This was one of her few pleasures; she scrimped dimes and quarters to take occasional voice and piano lessons. The throb of Caruso, so like the cantor's, reached out to her soul.

And—who knew?—filling the air with the tenor's voice might somehow make me sing like him.

These records in the early thirties cost two dollars each. Since my father earned about twenty-five dollars a week, laboring on piecework ten hours a day, each record meant half a day's efforts thrown away "just to hear an Eyetalyan scream!" Mamma kept these jewels in a closet, wrapped in old towels and quilts.

The goddamn Carusos revolved relentlessly on a hand-wound machine with a large brass horn. Mamma bought it secondhand, using money borrowed from her cousin, Abe Bernstein, who had become rich by owning a garment factory, not by working in one. He thought she was crazy. To me, the most insane folly was that she played Caruso so *loud*. And the windows were wide open in baseball weather.

I had nightmares of my pals turning their backs on me, with dirty winks, when they chose up sides. My life turned into a clear-cut fight; the block versus Mamma—the Dempsey-Tunney battles.

I'd shut the windows of the room facing the street, and my father would yell, "I'm dying—open the windows!"

"Oh, no," I said. "So much racket in the streets I can't hear this great music." And he'd raise the windows again.

The records and Mamma's drive for my future were intermingled with food—"Eat, eat, my genius"—so that by the time I was twelve I was a child prodigy.

I wore size forty pants. And I never could steal any bases. I also developed the hay-fever syndrome, although little ragweed could possibly grow in those fields of asphalt and cement. And somewhere along the way I managed to fall into stuttering in moments of tension. Mamma's reaction was characteristically accurate. "You're cutting off your throat to spite my face. It's all right. To be a mother is to suffer." I was the one who suffered: I was the st-tu-tu-tering f-f-f-atso who t-t-took the nee-needling on the b-b-block....

Mamma began to study English at night school. I thought this was a very progressive step: She might become interested in the outside world and stop bothering me. Until the Day the Piano Came.

The old dark-oak upright arrived in a truck from the Henry Street Settlement House, which had given it to her for only ten dollars. Nobody on the block had a piano, so a crowd gathered to debate how it would get up the sixth floor. Carry it up the stairway? Impossible.

Another truck pulled up, boldly proclaiming THE ORIGINAL AARON ABRAMOWITZ HAULING CO. A pulley was hauled up to the roof while the window panels were removed from our front room. The piano, cradled in a rope sling, floated up to yells of "They'll never make it!"

They did. The next day, a little bent-over German came to tune it....

We moved to Brownsville, into an area boasting the chic name of Crown Heights and a newly built apartment with heat and hot water. I started the eight grade in New Utrecht High School, which was an entirely different ball game. I didn't have the comforting embrace of the old block, the school was so crowded the boys sat on the radiators, and the English teacher mocked my stutter. My stomach churned in his class, and I hated the written homework. I was all alone, fat, at war with the world.

Coney Island: That's where the action was. Starting in spring, we wore bathing trunks instead of underwear to school so that after classes we could take the subway and go in for a swim. As twilight approached, we gathered under the boardwalk and sang, accompanied by a ukulele, love's old sweet songs that we'd picked up on the radio. We chose a position where the boards overhead were separated, so we could watch the girls parade by. Our lookout would signal the approach of the good-lookers, our voices swelled louder, and we were surrounded by them. The Young Communist League girls were not the best-looking, but they did follow the party line: from each according to her abilities, to each according to his needs. And as the sun slowly sank over Coney Island, the sands under the boardwalk became a make-out resort.

For everyone but Fatso. I consoled myself at a boardwalk stand with hot dogs and soda.

One day I took a positive step—I acquired a ukulele. I mentioned to my mother that my friends were making music, and, next day, there was the ukulele on my bed. Since only three chords were needed for accompaniment I quickly became the boardwalk troubadour, my soprano ringing out cleanly with the Crosby and Russ Columbo favorites. I remember the afternoon, the song, and moment in which my voice changed: "Everything I Have Is Yours." I took the melody down a half-tone, then another...and another. What a delicious feeling—I was a baritone, a *man* at fourteen and a half. I was singing "Everything" with Crosby's own whistle and hum when I saw, through the boardwalk slats above, a girl peering down at me in disbelief.

"Say, you fellas got a *radio* down there?"

Her question gave me the answer to changing my whole world. Crosby was a millionaire now, making movies, too, but he'd started in radio; so had Russ Columbo, and Dick Powell had begun as a crooner. A pulsating stream of images flowed over me; a network studio in New York, a Pierce-Arrow with uniformed chauffeur...apartment on Park Avenue, then Hollywood, spotlights lighting up the sky for a premiere at Grauman's Chinese...I'd have to swat the girls away. Of course, I'd have to lose twenty-five or thirty pounds. I came home fired up to follow Crosby on the Road to Riches.

"Mr. Glick," as he was usually called—not

"Glick" or "Harry"—was the hardware-store man who had the

distinction of still being unmarried in his thirties. In Brooklyn,

in this part anyway, everybody was married. But red-haired Mr.

Glick, able-bodied except for his myopia, seemed content to live

alone over his store on Avenue M frying his own fish and, when

business was slack, sitting out front in a camp chair taking the

sun and nodding to passersby with a wink and a barely percept-

ible ironic smile. His hardware business, probably because it

involved repairing things, managed to survive on a block of

Playwright

SHOESHINE BOYS OR "BOOT
BLACKS" AS THEY WERE
KNOWN IN THE EARLY 30s.
THESE BOYS LIVED IN THE
GOWANUS SHACK COLONY
IN WESTERN BROOKLYN.

A R T H U R

M I L L E R

failed, empty stores. I had already formed a deep connection to hardware and loved to hang around Mr. Glick, as did several other boys, especially Sammy the Mongoloid, who was probably Mr. Glick's closest friend. Sammy, also in his thirties then, knew every family in every house in those blocks of little houses, but not by name, only by phone number....

Merchants like Mr. Glick were spending a lot of time sit-ting out in front of their stores waiting for customers, but they were the lucky ones; wherever one walked FOR RENT signs were pasted across empty store windows, and there was hardly an apartment house without a permanent VACANCY sign on it. People were doubling up, married children returning to their parents with their own children. There were touch football games in the side streets between teams whose members were twenty or older, fellows with no jobs or even hopes for one anymore, playing the days away like kids and buying Camels or Luckies one cigarette at a time, a penny apiece, from Rubin the candy-store man on Avenue M. The normal rites of passage tended to be skipped over; when I graduated from Abraham Lincoln High School in 1932, mine was by no means the only family that failed to show up for the ceremony, nor did I expect them to attend. I knew that with my education at an end I was but another new young man on the long line waiting for work. Anyway, with a master's degree, as the saying went, you might get hired selling ties in Macy's.

If there was a national pastime I suppose it was hanging out, simply standing there on the street corner or on the beach waiting for something to appear around the bend. Evenings, before I had begun to feel embarrassed about any self-display, I'd be out there in front of Dozick's drugstore with half a dozen others singing the latest hits, sometimes in competition with anyone else who thought he sang better (for a couple of pennies you could buy pirated mimeoed lyrics of the newest songs). After I had turned fifteen these competitions seemed childish, but I continued as one of the star comics of the gang, improvising inanities, doing imitations of the Three Stooges, who even then were on the verge of our contempt as idiotic shadows of the Marx Brothers. We always had a sandlot football team going, and one of our half-

backs, a giant with a heavy lower lip named Izzy Lenowitz, whom nobody dared tackle for fear of his bowling ball knees, would clap me on my thin back and implore me, "Oh, come on, Artie, enjoy us." And with sufficient encouragement I would ad-lib a monologue that with a little luck might stay airborne for five minutes or more. Without plan or awareness of what I was doing, I had begun the process of separating myself: I was moving out of the audience to face them alone.

My mother and brother excepted...I cannot remember a person in the neighborhood who willingly read a book, there being no practical reason for doing so. The boys on those blocks had other things on their minds; mainly how to get girls, those innocent victims of male lust—in my day specifically Mary Costigliano, already near thirty, with enormous breasts and just possibly feebleminded, who was reported to fall stunned and helpless before anybody who brought her a box of Whitman's candy. True or not, this caused sniggers when she walked by, and occasionally she would stop in the street to scream at some insulting boy....

It was Brooks Atkinson's campaign for *All My Sons* that was responsible for its long run and my recognition as a playwright. And if I cannot prove it, I still believe that one of his motives in supporting the play and me was his concern that the New York theater be made hospitable to work that was not socially trivial. Had he not respected the

play, he would not have championed it, of course, but I think he used it as a lever to open the door to other voices that he hoped would come. In short, he was not oblivious to a responsibility for the whole theater enterprise....

We were living then in a converted brownstone on Pierrepont Street whose normal quiet was blasted one afternoon by a yelling argument in the hallway outside. Thinking violence was about to break out, I opened the door to find a small young man in army uniform sitting on the stairs with a young and beautiful woman whom I recognized as our upstairs neighbor. They went silent on seeing me, so I figured everything was in control and went back into our apartment. Later the young soldier, by now out of uniform, approached me on the street and introduced himself as a writer. His name, he said, was Mailer. He had just seen my play. "I could write a play like that," he said. It was so obtusely flat an assertion that I began to laugh, but he was completely serious and indeed would make intermittent attempts to write plays in the many years that lay ahead. Since I was at a time when I was hammering out my place in the world, I made few friends then, and Mailer struck me as someone who seemed to want to make converts rather than friends, so our impulses, essentially similar, could hardly mesh. (I am at the age when it is best to be charitable.) In any event, although we lived for years in the same neighborhood, our paths rarely crossed.

H E N R Y

He was the very first friend in my life. A

friend from the street, where we first met, in that glorious Four-

teenth Ward [in Brooklyn] I have written about so glowingly. We

were both five years of age. I had other little friends in that

neighborhood beside Stasiu of course. It has always been easy

for me to make friends. But Stasiu was my real friend, so to

speak, my pal, my buddy, my constant companion. Stasiu was

what his parents called him. None of us dared call him that

because it made him a "Polak," and he didn't want to be thought

of as a Polak. His name was Stanley and Stasiu is the affectionate

M I L L E R

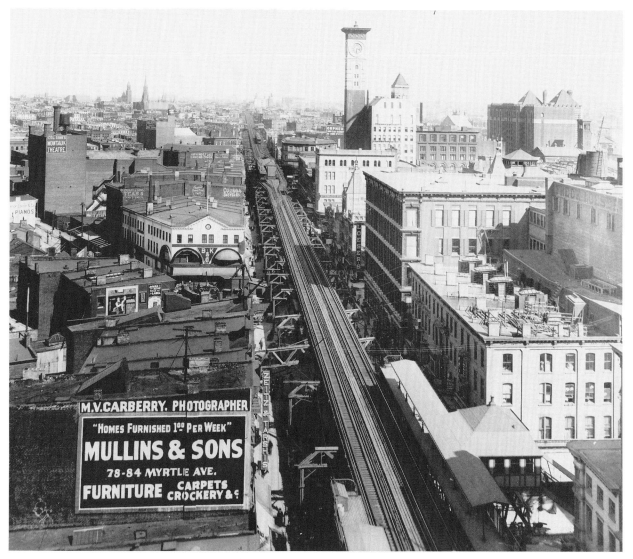

diminutive for Stanley. I can still hear his aunt calling in her sweet staccato voice—"Stasiu, Stasiu, where are you? Come home, it's late." I will hear that voice, that name until my dying day.

Stanley was an orphan who had been adopted by his aunt and uncle. His aunt, a woman of enormous proportions with breasts like cabbages, was one of the sweetest, kindest women I have ever known. She was a real mother to Stanley, probably much better than his own mother would have been had she lived. His uncle, on the other hand, was a drunken brute who owned the barbershop on the ground floor of the house we lived in. I have the most vivid and terrifying memories of him chasing Stanley through the streets with an open razor in his hand, cursing him at the top of his lungs and threatening to cut his head off.

Though Stanley was not his son, he, too, had an unbridled temper, particularly when one teased him. He seemed to have no sense of humor whatever, even later when he had grown up. Strange, now that I think of it, that "droll" was one of his favorite words. But that was much later, when he had dreams of being a writer and would write me lengthy letters from Fort Oglethorpe, of Chickamauga, when serving in the cavalry.

Certainly as a boy there was nothing droll about him. On the contrary, his expression was usually glum, morose, downright mean at times. If I angered him, as I did occasionally, he would chase after me with clenched fists. Fortunately I could always outrun him. But these chases were long and full of terror. We were about the same size and build, but he would beat me to within an inch of my life.

What I did on these occasions was to outdistance him and then hide somewhere for a half hour or so before sneaking home. He lived at the other end of the block in a shabby three-story building much the same as ours. I had to be very wary sneaking home, for fear he was still on the lookout for me. I didn't worry about meeting him the next day because these rages of his always subsided in due time. When we met it would be with a smile, a wry one from Stanley, and shake hands. The incident would be forgotten, buried—until the next time.

One might wonder how I be-

came such good friends with a kid like this, who in the whole was a rather unsociable lad. It's hard for me to explain myself, and perhaps it's best I don't try. Maybe even at that early age I felt sorry for Stanley, knowing he was an orphan, knowing his uncle treated him like a dog. His foster parents were poor too, much poorer than my parents. There were many things I owned, toys, tricycle, guns, and so on, to say nothing of the special privileges that were granted me, which made Stanley jealous and envious. He was particularly annoyed, I remember, because of the beautiful clothes I wore. It didn't matter to him that my father was a boss tailor, rather well-to-do for that time, who could afford to indulge his fancy. Myself, I was rather embarrassed and often ashamed of wearing such sumptuous raiment when all the kids I associated with were virtually in rags. These duds my parents thought looked so fetching on me, made me look like a little Lord Fauntleroy, which I hated. I wanted to look like the rest of the gang, not like some freak from the upper classes. And so, now and then, the other kids would jeer at me as I walked hand in hand with my mother, and call me a sissy, which made me wince. My mother, of course, was insensitive to these gibes and to my feelings as well. She probably thought she was doing me a great favor, if she thought about it at all.

Already, at that tender age, I had lost all respect for her. On the other hand, whenever I went

to Stanley's home and met his aunt, that delicious hippopotamus, I was in seventh heaven. I didn't realize it then, but what made me so happy and free in her presence was that she was affectionate, a quality I didn't know mothers were supposed to possess in dealing with their offspring. All I knew was discipline, criticism, slaps, threats—or so it seems as I look back on this stage of my life.

My mother, for example, never offered Stanley a huge slice of rye bread smeared with butter and sugar, as did Stanley's aunt when I visited his home. My mother's greeting to Stanley usually was: "Don't make too much noise and be sure to clean up when you've finished playing." No bread, no cake, no warm slap on the back, no "how's your aunt" or anything. Just don't make a nuisance of yourself was the idea she conveyed by her manner.

Stanley didn't come very often to my home, probably because he sensed the unfriendly atmosphere. When he did it was usually because I was convalescing from some illness. I had all the child's illnesses, by the way, from chicken pox to diphtheria, scarlet fever, whooping cough, the measles, and what not. Stanley never had any illness that I knew of. One couldn't afford to be ill in a poor family like his.

THE ELEVATED RAILROAD ON FULTON STREET CONNECTED BROOKLYN'S EASTERN RESIDENTS TO THE DOWNTOWN AREA.

153

A R T

Owner of the Cleveland Browns
football team

As often as I explain, my children still

don't understand how I learned to play ball on the streets of New

York City. Of course, their growing-up days were spent in a place

very different from Brooklyn. Their adolescent reality included

well-manicured parks and enormous flower gardens, while my

experiences included the outdoor stoop of our Borough Park

house and a flower garden concocted of a Breakstone Cheese

box sitting on the pantry windowsill. I vividly remember the

landscape of that box: it was a droopy flower barely standing in

the middle of the cement and brick. I've also become ac-

M O D E L L

THE MAGNIFICENT PROSPECT PARK BOATHOUSE, FIVE YEARS AFTER IT OPENED IN 1904. ITS DESIGN COMES FROM THE RENAISSANCE PALACES THAT LINE THE CANALS OF VENICE.

customed to their blank stares as I describe our stickball games, using bats made from broom handles to hit a "spaldeen," or when I recall the joy of pitching pennies, playing scully or kick the can. And, when I relate my big "nights on the town," which were fun-filled evenings at the neighborhood pool hall or

bowling alley, or just hanging out on the corner, I sense they're not impressed. Yet for those of us who've been there, the great heritage of the streets of Brooklyn leaves a lasting impression.

Although I spent many hours playing on the streets in Borough Park, my family background was

quite different from that of most families on the block. My father was a successful retailer, operating America's first chain of retail stores that sold radios and appliances. He took over my grandfather's Modell's store in the early 1920s and expanded it into a multi-store operation. Because of his early success, my young years included chauffeurs, Packard limousines, and family trips in the summer. But when the stock market crashed in 1929, all the trappings of his wealth abruptly disappeared. Left without his business, he went to work as a salesman for a wine company. Using the same energy and ambition that had made him a successful businessman, he worked himself up to the sales-manager position with yet another company. Unfortunately in 1939, when I was fourteen, he died suddenly in Austin, Texas. Because he was the sole bread-winner, my family's welfare rapidly deteriorated. Left pretty much penniless, the family soon fell on hard times and it became an enormous struggle for us to survive. The dramatic turn-around that my family experienced—the stock-market crash, the Depression, and then my father's death—was the exact opposite of how a normal success story is written. To help my family through the hard times, I took a job as an electrician's helper at the Bethlehem Steel shipyard near Bush Terminal.

While working in the shipyard, I continued attending classes at New Utrecht High School. Several of my friends who went to New Utrecht with me included guys like Buddy Hackett, Jack Carter and Robert

Merrill, who, like most of my friends, were working very hard to be successful. On the other hand, there were several guys I hung out with that ended up in Sing Sing. While I was going there, the New Utrecht basketball team had a German kid named Frido Frey, who was one of the best high-school basketball players in the city. Everyone was in awe of him and success was written all over him. He was a tremendous athlete and a great basketball player who eventually played in the pros. An especially memorable teacher at New Utrecht was Abe Fletcher, the school's basketball coach. He was a great man, a terrific instructor, and a guy who I liked to be around. He had a wonderful sense of humor and was someone who meant a great deal to me. I was deeply saddened to learn, many years later, that he had been mugged and killed in front of his house.

Since the age of seven, I've been a football fanatic. I loved taking the trolley to Ebbets Field to watch the Brooklyn Dodgers football team play.* My favorite teams were those that played in the mid-1930s, and my heroes included Ace Parker, Bruiser Kinard, the receiver Perry Schwartz, and the team's punter, Ralph Kerchival. A particularly rugged player was Earl "Father" Lumpkin, a brute from Georgia Tech. He was so tough he played without a helmet. For twenty-five cents and a G.O. card (a General Organization card was issued to every New York City high-school student, and it entitled you to discounts on books, sporting

events, etc.) my cousin and I would get a seat in the temporary bleachers behind the Brooklyn Dodgers bench. The best game of the year was the annual Thanksgiving Day game played between the Dodgers and the New York Giants, a game I never missed. When the Dodgers eventually went bankrupt due to lack of attendance, (there was no such thing as TV or radio revenue for the team owners back then), I switched my allegiance to the New York Giants. But it was those great afternoons I spent in Ebbets Field, watching my heroes play, which prompted me to dream that someday I would own a football team. It was a remote expectation, a boy's fancy, really, that was seeded in the fact that since I wasn't good enough to play the game, I might as well own a team. When I bought the Cleveland Browns in 1960, that notion became a reality.

Up until the time I moved to Cleveland in 1960, I maintained close ties to Brooklyn. Although I kept an apartment in Manhattan I spent a lot of time in Borough Park with my family and close friends. Many of those friends are still my closest friends today. Whenever they visit Cleveland or I go back to New York, we'll have lunch or dinner and reminisce about the great times we shared. Many of the old memories of Brooklyn— the Dugan's bakery truck, the rallying cry for a nickel ice-cream bar from the Good Humor man, or the roller-hockey games played with a wooden puck sawed from a branch log, are always a part of the conversation.

*The Brooklyn Dodgers football team was a National Football League franchise from 1930 until they folded in 1944. The team came to Brooklyn after John Dwyer purchased the Dayton (Ohio) Triangles, a founding team of the National Football League, and moved them to Ebbets Field.

BRUCE
"COUSIN BRUCIE"
MORROW

Nationally syndicated
CBS-Radio disk jockey

A surefire test to find out if someone's

from Brooklyn is to ask three things: What is stoopball? What is

hit the penny? What kind of sewer man were you? The sewer

question usually exposes the impostor. I, for one, was a three-

sewer man. I played with a couple of four-sewer men during my

days in Flatbush though I never saw a five-sewer man. Sewers

were the benchmarks for a kid's athletic prowess. These circular

manhole covers spaced approximately fifty feet apart in the

street easily measured how far you could hit a spaldeen. If you

were playing punchball, it was how far you could hit one with your fist. For stickball, where an old mop handle was used, the distance was always greater. It was important to be as high a sewer man as possible. A kid's stature in the neighborhood increased by the number of sewers he could hit a ball.

Life around East 26th Street, between V and W, included a slew of other activities besides stoopball, hit the penny, and stickball. A big neighborhood favorite was the empty-lot wars among the kids in the neighborhood. Early Saturday mornings our mothers would fill an empty Hellman's mayonnaise jar with milk or water, smear a glop of cream cheese and grape jelly (it had to be grape jelly!) on two pieces of Silvercup white bread, and send us out to war on the empty lots in the neighborhood. Our ammunition was the "dirt bombs" found in the lots, as well as branches and sticks. My East 26th Street compatriots would fight wars with the best armies East 19th Street, East 27th Street, and East 29th Street could muster. We'd fight these armies all day, except for the brief truce period for lunch, when we all ate together. By the end of the day, when we returned home, if our clothes weren't soiled with dirt and blood, our parents knew we didn't have a good time.

The Meyerowitz household was always the scene for some kind of commotion, and usually I was the cause for most of the chaos. Although we were mischievous children, my younger brother and I liked to help around the house, though what-

ever it was we tried to do usually ended up as a disaster. One evening as my parents prepared to go out, I overheard my mother commenting that the piano needed cleaning and tuning. As soon as they left, I told my brother to get the garden hose in the backyard. While he got the hose, I searched the laundry room for the Duz, Mom's favorite laundry detergent. We knew she would be proud of us as we emptied the Duz box into the paino, and on the count of three, opened up the hose nozzle full throttle. By the time we got done, the basement and the piano looked like a washing machine. We took a hell of a beating for that one, but I'm sure it was the cleanest piano in the neighborhood. In fact, wherever it is today, it's probably the cleanest instrument on the planet.

Another memorable episode was the Fourth of July Awning Incident. A couple of weeks before every July, I would venture into Chinatown to buy fireworks, and I would purchase everything from ash cans and roman candles to bottle rockets and whistling chasers. One year I learned my parents were planning to go to the Mayfair Theatre the night of the big celebration, so I sent a Rexograph announcement to all the neighbors, heralding the First Annual Meyerowitz Fireworks Display. Our East 26th Street neighbors knew that when the Meyerowitz boys did something, it usually turned into an event. They surely weren't going to miss the spectacle. As all the neighbors gathered to watch, we set up our

fireworks stand on the front porch, lining up three sky-rockets to start things off. With the whole block counting down, the first two rockets took off beautifully, causing everyone to ooh and aah in the street. The third rocket ignited, took off, and fizzled out halfway up, landing on the uppermost window canvas awning, setting it on fire. To make matters worse, the fire-ball awning drops down onto the porch awning, which itself goes up in flames! By the time my parents got home, the fire trucks were putting out the blaze, the street was empty, and my brother and I were hiding in a neighbor's house.

As adventurous as I was around the neighborhood, I was a very shy child in school and was always frightened when I was called upon to answer a question. The principal and teachers in P.S. 206 were very intimidating, so it wasn't until I got to James Madison High School that I began to feel more assured in the school environment. The teacher who helped me overcome my shyness was Mrs. Freilicher, an English teacher, who convinced me to try out for the school's annual hygiene play. High-school classes at that time weren't as progressive as they are today, the main issues being correct bathing and cleaning teeth. The plays were offshoots of class discussions. Consequently I won a part in the play, playing, of all things, a cavity. As soon as I went on stage and saw the audience respond to my lines, something happened: I fell in love with performing. As

luck would have it, about this same time I was recommended for the All-City Radio Workshop, held at Brooklyn Tech High School. Twice a week I traveled to the workshop as part of my English curriculum, and I received hands-on, on-the-air experience. Till this day I haven't forgotten what I learned there. The class produced educational plays with a moral story, reported the news, and made documentaries. It was a wonderful way to learn about radio, and it was a great time in my life.

159

Instead of going to a ball game, my father would take me for a walk on the boardwalk on Brighton Beach. We'd walk and talk on the boardwalk, and when we got tired he'd rent two beach chairs. If our walk was in the winter, we'd wrap ourselves in blankets as we sat in the chairs. We'd lie in the sun, with our eyes closed, holding reflectors to warm our faces, and talk about the world, my future, his business, and anything that came to mind. Those were wonderful, special times. I loved those talks, and when I walk along a boardwalk today, I think of those days in Brighton Beach.

Brooklyn people enjoy a special camaraderie that genuinely transcends that of all other places. There is an intangible glue that makes for our special affinity, a desire to live, a tradition of cohesiveness that binds us together. We're gritty people who know how to survive and flourish. Brooklyn teaches you to be on your toes, to be very aware of what's around you. The energy to excel comes from your family, friends, and classmates. The little boiler rooms of energy in Brooklyn were the schoolyards and the streets. It's there where we developed our skills, our cunning, daring, and learned how to survive in a competitive environment. As competitive as it was, if an outsider intruded into our world, we'd close ranks and fight together. Brooklyn was a wonderful world. For me, it's a magnet, a siren, that will always call out. But you can only hear the sound if you lived in Brooklyn.

HARRY

Singer and composer

The Bushwick neighborhood I grew up in

during the forties was a rough area teeming with lots of Irish, Italian, and black gangs. In order to survive, everyone in the area was tough, including the Jesuit brothers at Our Lady of Good Council School on Madison Street. I was born on June 15, 1941, in Bushwick Hospital and lived at 762 Jefferson Avenue, at the corner of Patchen Avenue. My father returned home from World War II with a permanent injury that was further complicated by an industrial accident. He eventually walked out on the family when I was very young, and ended up living on a pension

NILSSON

most of his life. My mother married five more times, so my younger sister and I were raised with lots of stepfathers. Because my mother worked nights as a waitress in the Waldorf-Astoria, and I was going to Our Lady of Good Council grammar school during the days, we didn't see much of each other. So, besides the stepfathers, my grandmother and an aunt and uncle were in charge of keeping an eye on me during the day.

The neighborhood was always filled with violence, and fights in the street were common between the Halsey Street gang and the gang from Patchen Avenue. The gangs had their turf to protect and fighting was a way to defend what they owned. Sooner or later, whether you liked it or not, the violence would touch your life. One of my earliest memories is a summer evening hanging out on a stoop and seeing a guy get shot in the neck with a zip gun. The shooting took place right in front of me. I saw the guy clutch his neck as he fell to the ground and I became

WORKERS SPILLING OUT ON THE
GROUNDS OF THE BROOKLYN NAVY
YARD TO CELEBRATE COMPLETION
OF A SHIP. THE USS *Missouri*,
USS *Iowa* AND THE AIRCRAFT
CARRIER *FDR* WERE ALL BUILT IN
BROOKLYN.

frightened beyond belief.
While still a youngster, I was
forcibly recruited by a gang for a
street rumble. I was told to go up
on the roof of a Jefferson Avenue
building and wait for the other
gang to appear. When I hesitated
at first, the leader threatened
me. You just didn't say no to
these guys. They armed us with
rocks, sticks, and bottles and
sent us up to wait. At the appropriate signal we were to throw
down our street ammo on the opposing gang. After a short time,
I could see both gangs slowly appear on the street. Peering over
the side, I felt the tension of the
impending rumble. One gang
stalked along Patchen Avenue

while the other came up Jefferson. The movements of the gangs
positioning themselves on the
streets were similar to maneu-
vers of opposing armies readying
for war. I watched as both gangs
closed in on each other. To this
day I can remember where both
gangs crashed. They collided
right in front of my house! I
waited for the signal, but there
was so much chaos and hysteria
on the street that, when it finally
came, I was confused about who
to throw my ammunition at. I
halfheartedly threw down what I
had in my hand and hurried off
the roof.

As brutal as the gangs on the
streets were, they were equally
matched by the priests and
brothers at Our Lady of Good
Council. The school was run like
a prison and, because it was a
Catholic school, the boys and
girls were separated by a high
fence. During the school day the
boys weren't allowed to talk to or
even see the girls. Discipline was
extremely tight. Order and rules
were strictly applied and harshly
enforced. Anyone stepping out of
line or caught fooling around
was severely punished. Many
times a kid was beaten for com-
mitting a small infraction. One
brother would hit us with a stick,
sometimes for no apparent reason. I have very bad memories of
this guy. He once savagely beat a
classmate because the kid didn't
understand a question. The class
sat in shocked silence as the
beating went on. It was an awful
experience. Another memorable
event during my years in Our
Lady of Good Council was the
day a howling hurricane passed

through Brooklyn. Trees were
uprooted, garbage cans were
tossed all over the streets, the
big oak tree that stood in the
graveyard across from our house
was knocked down, and the high
fence separating the boys and the
girls had been ripped apart from
the heavy wind. For several days,
while the fence was being re-
paired, we finally had an
opportunity to see the girls. The
strict, regimental code of the
school was temporarily broken
and the whole school reveled in
delight.

During the years imme-
diately after the end of World
War II, great convoys of military
apparatus would rumble through
Bushwick on their way to the
Brooklyn Navy Yard. According
to the newspapers, much of the
military hardware stored at the
Navy Yard was to be shipped to
American bases around the
world. When a convoy was sched-
uled to thunder through
Bushwick, the whole neighborhood would eagerly filter onto
the streets and wait with great
excitement.

After hours of waiting, a
great display of military trucks,
jeeps, half-tracks, tanks, and
soldiers began to appear. The
neighborhood got a special thrill
watching this impressive parade
marching through their streets. I
sensed that it temporarily
brought the neighborhood together in some small way.
Although many of the spectators
grew bored and left after a short
while, my fascination with this
mighty spectacle never dwindled
until the very last tank rumbled
by.

Even though both my parents were born

and grew up in Brooklyn, our home was quite Italian in atmosphere. That means we spoke with flying hands as well as competing voices, especially when my mother's six sisters and three brothers all piled in to visit at the same time and outshout one another. When Mom's parents came, the vocabulary respectfully shifted to Italian. My mother didn't encourage us kids to learn Italian, however, because our neighborhood was mostly Irish, German, and Jewish. She was fervent that outsiders not think of us as a family of wops. Mothers of the other kids from

JOE PATERNO

the other groups, each with its own cruel name—mick and kraut and Jew-boy—had the same fears for their kids. That was New York in those days.

Yet ethnic identity was important, almost like your name. Where we lived, when a kid asked, "What are you?" he didn't mean are you a second baseman or a baritone. He meant, "Are you Irish or German or Italian or Jewish or what?" Religion—just having one, and believing your religion was the truth—was important, too, even if yours wasn't the same as the other guy's. When a Jewish kid had to abandon the stickball game to get to *shul* on time on the High Holy Days, the rest of us understood. And in those days I felt chosen when that kid's family asked me in to light their stove because they weren't supposed to strike matches. I was the *Shabas goy*. Of course, everybody knew your family was important to you, and you assumed the other kid's family was important to him....

Often all our relatives with all their kids gathered in one place, say at my Uncle John's house in Coney Island. Uncle John had once been a policeman. He stood as upright as the Empire State Building and expected us to do the same. After Sunday dinner, he'd pair us up, more or less according to age and size, and we had to go at each other in boxing matches. At six years old, I was defending myself boxing. Uncle John "taught" us all to swim. He'd lead us all out to the end of the ocean pier and throw us in, one by one. The choice was to swim or die. While I learned I could swim, I never again had an urge to go leaping into the ocean.

Uncle John had a plumbing business, and he gave some of my cousins summer work at good money, two dollars for up to a fourteen-hour day, usually for the dirty jobs. I tried it for one day and never asked for more....

My mother had us move from house to house a lot, to be near one of her six sisters, then another, and another, but all the moves were in the same general section of Brooklyn. One was a house we rented on 23rd Street between Avenue S and Avenue T, near St. Edmond's. It was a nice street, lots of playing room, lots of kids to play with, and we played all day in summer, all afternoon the rest of the year. Playing daily at sports was our work: not only touch football, but also punchball and stickball, using a high-bounce ball made by A.G. Spalding Company, which any street kid knew was called a *spaldeeeen*. At stickball, when the wind was right, I could hit a two-and-a-half sewers. (Anybody who needs that ex-

plained never lived in New York.)

One really important guy on the block, an adult, was named Jack Smith. What made him important was not his family, or his religion, or his ethnic group, none of which I knew anything about. He was a famous *sports* writer—and for the greatest, most important information medium of any kind anywhere in the entire world, the *New York Daily News*. On almost any day of the week, you could see his *name* there, at the top of articles he actually wrote. But that wasn't half of why we valued him as a neighbor. One of his good friends—he knew him *personally*—was Tommy Heinrich of the New York Yankees, who every afternoon played the outfield beside Joe DiMaggio and George Selkirk. More than once, Jack Smith came walking from the subway station just a couple of hours after a game, bringing Tommy Heinrich himself home for dinner. We might have heard his name on the radio that very day, hauling down a spectacular catch, or parking one in the upper deck, and here he was on 23rd Street! Jack Smith would introduce him to each one of us by our names, and then Tommy Heinrich would throw us a few passes. I couldn't imagine any greater thrill, except his being a Brooklyn Dodger instead of a Bronx Bomber. I'd go to bed with goose bumps from the excitement.

When I was finishing St. Edmond's, we had moved to 26th and Avenue R, just one block from James Madison High

School, a very good public school. At the bus stop on our corner, James Madison kids unloaded every morning by the hundreds. I guess I expected to become one of them, but my dad said, "No, I want you to go to a Catholic school." That meant he'd have to pay tuition of twenty bucks a month. At today's dollar, that might correspond to two hundred bucks a month or more. He had to take an extra job for it. Never once did I hear my parents say, "We can't afford to send you."

My father enrolled me at Brooklyn Preparatory School, run by Jesuits....A year and a half later, [my brother] George was to go to St. Augustine's, a diocesan high school that was very good and where he'd have a cost-free scholarship. By the time George was ready to go, I had begun playing football at Brooklyn Prep. St. Augustine's didn't have football. George pleaded that if he could go to Brooklyn Prep, too, he'd play his heart out at football and win a college athletic scholarship. My father went to see the headmaster, Father John Hooper, and struck a deal for us both to go to Brooklyn Prep at a cut rate. So now he had to put up thirty bucks a month. After my dad died and I had to get all his financial records in order, for the first time I got a full view of what my parents went without to give us what we had. He died with empty pockets.

JOAN

During my entire childhood, from the be-

ginning, my father was constantly struggling to catch up to [the

family's] debts, but my sister Barbara and I always had those

governesses, had the clothes, the piano lessons, the best private

schools in Brooklyn with tuitions way beyond our means, first at

Brooklyn Ethical Culture School and then Adelphi Academy,

where I transferred after the sixth grade.

As at Brooklyn Ethical, I endured a periodic ritual at Adel-

phi. I walked down the shallow half steps of the huge pink mar-

ble staircase, holding on to the high, polished wooden

RIVERS

balustrade, my body stiff and
awkward with fright. At the
bottom I crossed the wide marble
entrance hall toward the school
office, which had windows facing
into the hall, and I could see the
two secretaries and the headmaster, Mr. Amos, at his desk. I
went into the office and
everybody looked at me and I
could tell they *knew.* I had to
say, "Please, can I speak to Mr.
Amos," and I was sent into the
inner office and Mr. Amos
looked at me and I handed him
the tuition check, saying, "My
mother said to leave this and
could you please hold it for two

weeks. Thank you very much." Added to my humiliation was the terror that he would say, "We don't want you in the school anymore." Sometimes he answered, "Tell your parents we can hold it only one week." And whenever I passed Mr. Amos in the hall, I knew *he* knew that I could not afford to be there. Of course, I believed I was the only child in the whole school who could not afford it. Sometimes the check would bounce, and I would be called down to Mr. Amos's office and he would say, "Please say to your parents that the check did not go through and that we are going to redeposit it tomorrow." So I had to go home with that message, that knowledge. I always thought that I *had* to deliver those checks.... But I understand now: headmasters cannot yell at a six-year-old. Or an eight-year-old. Or a thirteen-year-old....

Now that I was at Adelphi, my father drove me each morning and often delivered me to school late. In front of the entire student body I had to walk up the three steps to the teacher's desk and bend over and sign the late book with my rear end toward the room—and I knew it was a big rear end and everybody was looking at the nerd's hips. I kept trying to walk in sideways, because you can suck in your stomach, but I defy anybody to suck in hips. After about a week I told my mother I was miserable, told her that when I had to change into my gym uniform in front of everybody, my thighs were twice as big as Marilyn Abrams's hips and Jane

Weissman's whole body could fit in my one arm. She told me, "When they find out you are a lovely girl from a lovely background, everything will turn around." Unfortunately, nobody ever checked our house.

In the first three years at Adelphi, from the seventh grade through high-school freshman, I had almost no girlfriends. At lunchtime, I never knew whether there was a place for me at the table and always put my tray down so tentatively—not the way Marilyn Abrams or Jane Weissman did, or Frances Rothman, who could put her tray down anywhere and people were happy to have her. Boys were distant, impossible mysteries. I knew only one thing about them. I knew I had nothing they wanted, that no boy was ever waiting for me, no valentine was ever in the box with my name on it. I tried to convince myself that looks were not important, that what mattered was the inner me, but boys did not like my personality either. I was doomed to yearn from afar, writing in my diary, "Eliot sits near Delia in science. Of all the luck! I sit near Alice." Then, cruel as only kids can be, Eliot wrote in my yearbook, "Ashes to ashes, dust to dust; Joan is a girl with a forty-inch waist." Well, that ruins your yearbook—you cannot show it to anybody....

School dances were always disasters. When my father arrived home from delivering me, he never took off his shoes or undressed. He waited on red alert, knowing that within an hour there would be a call saying,

"Come get me." But I was a stupid optimist and each week I would forget my awkwardness, the sick misery in the stomach that afflicts nerds, and would get all dressed up again for the next dance, hoping this time I would be acceptable—only to be taught, yet again, that I was still a pig.

I remember in particular Jane Weissman's party. She was a hot girl at Adelphi, an apprentice vamp who played the guitar and was thin and had long hair that flipped under and wore lipstick and deodorant. She invited the whole class to a costume party and my mother decided I should go as a Russian girl. She put me, four feet eight and 120 pounds, into a red turtleneck and dirndl skirt and embroidered an old hat with pearls and ribbons that hung down the back. We found boots. She *really* thought I was going to a costume party and I absolutely thought I was going to be fine in that getup.

Of course, on the big night everybody else was in togas and skimpy little Daisy Mae costumes—and I marched in as Mother Russia. Nobody danced with me. When we played spin the bottle, I went into the dark room with a boy who right away said, "Let's forget this," and the next time in the room another boy took my nose and twisted it, which makes you realize you are not attractive. So I sat in Jane's kitchen and played with her dogs and called my father to come and get me.

I was four years old when we moved to

Grand Avenue in Bedford-Stuyvesant, and I was raised by devout

Baptist parents who came to Brooklyn from North Carolina in

early 1929. We were farm people who came north looking for

Critically acclaimed jazz
drummer and composer

better days, but soon after we arrived the stock market crashed.

Religion played a major role in the family, and the Concord

Baptist Church on the corners of Clinton and Marcy avenues,

was interwoven in our daily life-style. I spent many hours in that

church, because in addition to offering spiritual enlightenment,

it was active in many other ways. It served as a community day-

MAX
ROACH

care center we'd go to after school. There were arts and crafts, musical instruments, and other activities to keep us busy. It also presented speakers to address the congregation on political, cultural, and economic affairs, inviting people like Paul Robeson, for example, to offer their commentaries on the human condition. Because times were especially hard, the church set up a credit union for parishioners who didn't have jobs or couldn't borrow money from the local bank. Concord Baptist was the place I spent my weekend time, too. On Sundays it was a day-long affair. I'd first attend religious school, followed by morning service, after which I'd have an afternoon dinner in the church with my family and other parishioners. We'd end the day by attending yet another service in the evening. I remember saying to myself that when I got older, I wasn't going to spend so much time in church. But I'm still a member of Concord Baptist today.

Religious music permeated the household. Indeed, my interest in music was sparked by my family's activities in church. My mother was a passionate gospel singer and my aunt played the piano during church services. Although my aunt taught and continued to encourage me to play the piano, it was a marching-band bugle that paved the way to my musical destiny. A teacher in my elementary school gave me a bugle to learn for the school band. But when I took it home, I couldn't get a sound out of it. After several frustrating

hours, my mother gently suggested I take it back and get something I could handle. The next day I came home with a snare drum and immediately fell in love.

Another phenomenon that enhanced my musical interests were the "house rent" parties that were prevalent in Bedford-Stuyvesant. These parties took place during the early thirties right after the crash, when times were really difficult for people. A common sight of the times was seeing a family's belongings out on the street, a sign of eviction. When a family couldn't make ends meet, the solution was to throw a "house rent" party, whereby neighborhood musicians came to the family's house and had a session. An admission fee was charged to the neighbors, usually a nickel or a dime, and beer and other refreshments were served. The money the family raised from the party paid the month's rent. The parties became a custom in the neighborhood. As a young child, going to a "house rent" party was very exciting. The glamour of the musicians was larger than life and I remember curiously touching their instruments, the saxophones, the drum set, the bass fiddle and trumpets. Best of all was the music they played. They played music called jazz and the blues, sounds you didn't hear in church. The driving rhythms and haunting melodies of this music reverberated in many Bedford-Stuyvesant living rooms in the 1930s.

Although my parents were devout churchgoers and spirited

gospel singers, they did appreciate the sounds of other music. As I became more involved with music, they never showed a resistance to my interest in jazz. My desire to play music other than gospel, though, was the cause for ending a relationship with a teenage crush. Her name was Betty Staten. Betty, along with my sports and music-pursuits, was the biggest interest in my life. Many evenings I'd go over to her house and we'd sit in her living room and talk. One day her father came in, sat down, and asked me what I wanted to do with my life. I announced proudly: "I want to be a jazz musician." It was the wrong thing to say. Betty's father was a church minister who frowned on jazz and the blues. He was a strict Baptist who accepted only gospel music that celebrated God. After that conversation, Betty went right out of my life.

As a young teenager, I hung out with a couple of guys who would someday make a name for themselves in the jazz world. We'd hang out at the local candy store owned by Randy Weston's father. Randy played a great piano, and, along with Randy and Cecil Payne, I spent many hours talking endlessly about the music we'd hear on the radio. We'd listen to Cab Calloway, Louis Armstrong, Billy Johnson, and the Count Basie Band from Chicago. There were many jazz bands playing at that time. Brooklyn had its own Apollo Theater, and all the bands that played the Apollo in Manhattan would come to the Brooklyn Apollo. The Apollo and the

Brooklyn Paramount booked great bands to play their stages, and we'd bring lunches and spend all day listening to jazz and the big-band sounds.

My first gig playing jazz in front of an audience was in between halves of a high-school basketball game. We played for many of these cafés, playing in places like the Old Elks Bar on Wilson Street or the Sonya Bar on Bedford Avenue. Another popular place to play was the dime-a-dance clubs. For a dollar, a guy would get ten dances with the women who were on the dance floor. We'd play one thought that I could roll out the front door of my apartment, go around the corner, and sit in at one of the local clubs. It was a wonderfully vibrant time.

the crowd during halftime and received very little money. In those days, seventy-five cents could buy a complete arrangement for a big band from the local music store. We'd use these scores as our charts. Gradually we began playing dances where we got a couple of dollars a night. As I improved and got older, I started to play the local bars and clubs. Those days were still prejukebox, so every bar, café, or club would have a piano for entertainment. I'd get a call to accompany the piano player in chorus and stop. The guys on the floor would tear off one of their ten tickets from the roll and give it to the girl he was dancing with. We then played another chorus, and another ticket was torn. And on it went. I played a lot of dime-a-dance gigs with Bud Powell, one of the best jazz pianists ever. There was music on just about every corner in Brooklyn back then. So many places were offering so much music—jazz, big-band, and blues. I was thrilled to be a part of it. What I loved most was the

THE BROOKLYN BRIDGE WALKWAY CONNECTING BROOKLYN WITH LOWER MANHATTAN. IF YOU DIDN'T WANT TO WALK YOU COULD DRIVE OR TROLLEY OVER THE BRIDGE.

173

NBC-TV weatherman

The Seaview Projects complex, which

towers over the Belt Parkway in Canarsie, epitomized the melting-pot flavor of Brooklyn of the 1950s. The variety of nationalities who lived there were all bonded by their lower-middle-class status, yet the enduring hope for most families was owning their own home. To achieve that goal, parents sacrificed and worked very hard. While many families were able to move on, there were those who remained. I spent my early childhood years in the yellow tower in the Seaview Projects, the oldest child of Al and Isabel Roker. While there were occasional problems in

AL ROKER, JR.

the projects, it was basically a harmonious environment where people watched out for each other.

Because my father worked for many years as a bus driver for the New York City Transit Authority, some of my fondest memories of Brooklyn were the sights and sounds of his depot. Located on the site of the old Jackie Gleason Bus Depot, this cavernous, huge building had a Runyonesque quality that made it very enchanting. As a child, I looked forward to my visits, fascinated by the bustling activity that took place there. I was captivated by the official green uniforms of the bus drivers and the sight of disabled buses hanging on the lifts, attended to by grease-smeared mechanics. Equally alluring were the sounds of the locker doors clanging open and shut and the glow of the lighted offices on the second floor overhead.

The place was full of activity. On a typical afternoon, a crowd of bus drivers huddled around a card game in a distant corner, an odd-looking fellow took last-minute bets on the ponies, or a small-time hoodlum tried to peddle some cheap merchandise. There'd be guys singing, swearing, and kidding around. Pinup calendars adorned some of the lockers and occasionally I'd be treated to an ice cream or candy by a bus-driver friend of my father's. The most appealing sound I was attracted to through all this commotion was the incessant jingle of the bus drivers' change makers. The cadence of those

change makers, as they were emptied for the day, gave the depot a certain rhythm. I loved to hear the sounds of those change makers and was awed by the silver coins that spilled out. The most coveted possession I owned as a child was my father's old change maker. He gave it to me after he was issued a newer model. I'd wear that change maker on my belt and loved to play with it all day. It was a magical and wonderful toy.

On my days off from school and many days in the summer, I accompanied my father as he drove his route. At that time he was assigned to the B35 line, which traveled along Flatbush Avenue. All the passengers knew him by his first name and I was very proud as I watched him commiserate with the commuters. I'd ride the full eight-hour shift with him and the highlight of the day was the egg cream, sandwich, or comic book he'd buy me at the local luncheonette. We'd spend his lunch hours eating together in that Flatbush Avenue luncheonette or in the hushed quiet of his empty bus.

The first year in school didn't start out too well. My drawing creations in an art class at Canarsie's P.S. 272 caused quite a reaction from several of my school teachers. The year I entered kindergarten, psychological testing was in vogue and apparently the teachers picked up on an underlying problem in my five-year old personality through my artwork. Affecting a very serious tone, they called my parents and asked for a con-

ference "regarding Albert." My artwork, as analyzed by these teachers, indicated a very low self-esteem. As proof, the teachers pointed to several pictures I had drawn. They noted the difference between the very small size of me in the picture and the enormous size of the buildings, trees, and sky. My father, who has an art background, and knows all about the sense of perspective, grew impatient with their amateur psychology, and wanted to tell them they were wasting his and their time. He knew I was a well-adjusted boy who was drawing the world through five-year-old eyes. Thankfully my mother was the better diplomat, and she satisfied the teacher's concerns by suggesting a talk with me when they returned home. When they asked me why I had drawn such a huge house and expansive sky, I explained to them our house seemed high to me (it was a ten-story apartment building). That immediately put an end to my psychological analysis.

Once I got by my kindergarten art class, and began full-time first-grade classes, I began patronizing Moe the Knish Man. Moe was the local vendor who sold knishes from his cart in front of P.S. 272. For ten cents you'd get the best-tasting knish in Brooklyn, featuring a tasty, almost hard crust that encased a soft, fluffy potato texture on the inside. Moe's knishes looked like big, soft pillows, and till this day I have yet to taste a knish that's as good. Moe was always generous to the kids. If you didn't have a dime, Moe had what looked like a fifty-five gallon drum of salt next to his cart, from which he'd scoop up a handful and sprinkle it into your hand. In a way, he became part of the school's culture. The hallways were filled with kids walking to class while licking their hands.

Although I wasn't much for outdoor activities or sports—I have the distinction of falling on my face tripping over a Pensky Pinky (the poor cousin of the spaldeen)—I did enjoy some of the activities that took place around the projects. One special day was Halloween. As a kid canvassing apartments in the projects on Halloween, you could literally clean up in one building. If you were really fast, and started trick-or-treating early in the day, you might be able to get to the next building, but generally by that time you were pooped. To add to their efficiency, the kids in the buildings would set up an intelligence network, passing on strategic information on who was giving out what. If Mrs. McKay on the third floor was handing out quarters, you'd be sure every kid in the apartment building would be knocking on her door. On the flip side, if someone was a little on the cheap side with his treat, the kids wouldn't even waste their time. Because some of my best memories revolve around food, Halloween was a special day at the Seaview Projects and an occasion I always cherished.

A SIGN AT THE FOOT OF BAY PARKWAY ANNOUNCES THE CONSTRUCTION OF THE CIRCUMFERENTIAL PARKWAY. BECAUSE THE NAME WAS TOO AWKWARD TO PRONOUNCE, IT WAS LATER CHANGED TO THE BELT PARKWAY.

Movie critic

There was a perpetual feeling of aliena-

tion that enshrouded my family during my childhood in

Brooklyn. To capture the essence of that estrangement today, I

use a one-liner that always gets a chuckle: my parents were prob-

ably the only relief family in Brooklyn who voted for Alf Landon

in the 1936 election. My father was a proud immigrant from

Greece who detested Roosevelt and his New Deal, because he felt

Roosevelt's programs stripped dignity away from the working-

man. My father's politics were very Eurocentric; he talked about

America and "Americans" as if *they* were the aliens. Because we

ANDREW SARRIS

didn't associate with other immigrant Greek families, knew very little about our neighbors, and had no social life with my mother's side of the family because they were at odds with my father, we were a close-knit family that was out of sync with everyone else.

The Depression caught up to my family in 1931. Prior to that my father was a prosperous real-estate broker who owned many lots in Brooklyn. When the Depression hit, instead of Sunday afternoons driving through Brooklyn in a shiny Pierce-Arrow, we grudgingly turned to relief for help. As ironic as it may sound, it seemed a lot easier to be poor back then. My mother always had food on the table, and in those day's a landlord would give a relief family the first month's rent free when they leased an apartment. We would usually skip the next two months rent and subsequently get kicked out. Whereupon we would move on to a new apartment and start the cycle over again.

One place I vividly recall was our second-story apartment at 1533 Flatbush Avenue, on the corner of Nostrand Avenue. It was over a bookstore and a hardware store. Viewed through a child's eye, a hardware store is a fascinating place to visit. Often I'd go downstairs and walk through the store, marveling at the various colors, shapes, and packages of the goods on the shelves. These images came to mind decades later when I was visiting an art exhibit entitled *Hardware Store* in Canada. The exhibit featured hammers with dangling price tags, paint cans, carpenter saws, etc. I was amused that, at the age of six, I was into pop art long before I knew what it was!

Further manifestation of my father's antagonistic life-style was how we integrated with our neighbors culturally. We rooted against every popular team, professional or college, and all the top sports heroes. I cheered against the Yankees and the Dodgers at a time in New York when those two teams were held in godlike awe. My favorite team was the Detroit Tigers. I fell in love with the Tigers because I was taken in with photos of the Tigers' Mickey Cochrane and Charlie Gehringer that appeared on the back of a Kellogg's cereal box. We passionately rooted against Notre Dame, a very popular team at the time, and we favored Schmeling over Louis in their title fights. Such was life in the Sarris household.

One thing we did share with other families was the joy of going to the beach. From our apartment in Brooklyn, we first traveled on the trolley to Avenue U. From there, a ferry ride crossed the channel to Riis Park, where the salty sprays of the cool shore air were a welcome relief from the heat of the hot Brooklyn summer. The family had lots of fun at the beach. We also enjoyed going to Prospect Park for the parades that were staged for each holiday. One parade that comes to mind involved Mayor La Guardia and was held on Avenue D, in front of an apartment we were living in at the time. La Guardia was sched-uled to appear because he was making the rounds for his reelection. The day before the parade, a contingent of workmen arrived to set up several play facilities—monkey bars, seesaws, and slides—for the neighborhood kids. We were all very excited. The parade comes through, La Guardia makes his appearance, and several months later he's re-elected. The very next day after the election, the workmen return and dismantle the park. The neighborhood kids were in shock. I'll always remember that incident as my first taste of poli-tics in action.

Several of the grammar schools I attended were contrasts in architectural styles, some-thing that impressed me as a kid growing up. The very first school I attended, P.S. 152, was a beautiful American Renaissance building that looked like a medieval castle. Though I loved the look of that school, I never performed well there. I was very sickly during those first years in grammar school, and because I spoke Greek before I learned English, I constantly fell behind in my studies. When we moved to Avenue D and my mother en-rolled me into P.S. 89, things got better.

Unlike the beauty of P.S. 152, P.S. 89 was an ugly building that looked like a factory. It was at this school I met Miss Tobias, a dedicated and passionate teacher who cared for all her students. The class was a real melting pot, so Miss Tobias took the time to get to know our indi-vidual histories. She conducted private interviews with us and asked about our family background. Everyone in class felt very attached to Miss Tobias, and she helped bring us closer together. In certain ways, children were less aware about racial differences back then. The day the *Hindenburg* crashed was especially traumatic for a German girl in my class, and she cried incessantly. For many days after the crash, she was comforted and received sympathy from many kids in the class.

One of my favorite passions was going to the movies, though I never thought for a moment that someday films would be my business. The one movie theater I always wanted to go to was the Loews Kings, because I was impressed with its majestic architecture. Unfortunately, because the Kings charged more money, we went to the Rialto, Farragut, and Glenwood. Though I enjoyed my times at these other movie houses, it was the Loews Kings, with its noble marquee, and its beautifully designed American Renaissance style that I coveted. I remember when *Showboat* opened at the Loews Kings. Amid all the fanfare, gleaming lights, and excitement, I pressed my face up against the door of the theater, sneaking a wondrous peek at its interior. Thirty years later as I settled in to watch *Showboat* at a distant movie theater, the Loews Kings with its grand and ornate design, a style that symbolized the whole idea of extravagance, escapism, and exoticism—the perfect setting for a movie— came to mind.

While my father set the tone

regarding family politics and our relations to outsiders, my mother was the force that held us together as a family unit. She was a strict and stern parent while raising me and my brother, but at the same time she had great sensitivity. She harshly admonished us one day when she caught us cruelly teasing a kid on the block. I quickly realized she had a sensitivity that reached beyond her children, an empathy that I had never seen before in other mothers. I came to this conclusion through personal experience. I remember taking an awful beating by an Irish kid who was the bully in the neighborhood. His mother suddenly came along, and in between punches, I noticed her smiling approvingly at her superior son. She never raised a hand or uttered a word to stop the slaughter. My mother's tenderness also helped temper the poverty we experienced during the Depression years. One Christmas morning, while we were living on Avenue D, my brother George and I woke up and went downstairs to an empty storefront where my mother had set up a Christmas tree. My father was totally broke, so we didn't expect much, if anything, for Christmas. To our amazement, there sat the largest supply of gifts we'd ever received. To add to the celebration, my mother invited all the neighbors in to enjoy the Christmas tree, and we ended up having a terrific holiday in the little storefront on Avenue D.

There was a sense of community during those years, a feeling

that doesn't exist today in Brooklyn, or anywhere else, for that matter. There was much less money, food, and clothing back then, although it seems more things were shared. Social life was more courteous, a certain plebeian *politesse* existed. Brooklyn was like a commonwealth, a colony of peoples, yet at the same time it served as a gateway. It was a starting point for families to get back on track after the Depression and move on with their lives.

TOP: A CONTINGENT OF CIVIL DEFENSE WARDENS POSE ON THE ROOFTOP OF THEIR FLATBUSH APARTMENT BUILDING. ABOVE: THE SPECTACULAR FACADE OF P.S. 152 ON GLENWOOD ROAD.

DICK

ABC-TV sportscaster and
best-selling author

Abe Stark's HIT SIGN, WIN SUIT advertise-

ment in Ebbets Field looked a lot different from home plate that

hot summer day in 1949. In my adolescent years I saw that

famous sign from the stands when my father took me to the

Dodger games. Now here I was a fifteen-year-old first baseman

with the Freeport, Long Island, Barons in the New York State

Kiwanis League, playing for the state championship in

Brooklyn's grandest baseball setting. I had moved from

Brooklyn with my family some time before, but that day I step-

ped into the batter's box at Ebbets Field proved to be a dream

SCHAAP

fulfilled, a fantasy every Brooklyn-born street kid dreamed. I don't recall how I hit that day. Although I had a high batting average, most of my hits were bunts, not the frozen-rope line drives you'd see the Dodgers occasionally smack. But that didn't matter. The thrill of returning to Brooklyn and playing in that grand ball park is something I'll never forget. Winning the New York State Kiwanis League championship was icing on the cake.

My family moved to Long Island via the Flatbush route. I was born in Beth Israel Hospital into a long line of Brooklynites, many of whom attended Erasmus Hall High School. My mother and father attended Erasmus, as did my uncles, aunts, and all my cousins. Erasmus Hall tradition permeated the household. After we left Brooklyn, I kept track of Erasmus's teams while living in Long Island and Florida. My Brooklyn roots began in a house on Linden Boulevard, but soon after, my family settled into a two-story brownstone on East 31st Street between Avenue D and Cortelyou. We lived down

A "MODERN" ONE-MAN FLATBUSH AVENUE TROLLEY WITH THE WILLIAMSBURGH SAVINGS BANK IN THE BACKGROUND.

the block from my grandparents' house. One of my favorite things to do when I was a boy was explore Farragut Woods. We'd spend hours in those woods, playing all kinds of games and top off the day's events by roasting mickeys in the ground. Potatoes never tasted the same after you had the luxury of tasting a mickey. We'd wash down those mickeys with anything we could snatch from our parents' refrigerators.

Like many households of the era, radio played a big part in our lives and it was a special treat for me to tune into Mayor La Guardia reading the funnies. My parents held liberal views so their favorite radio show was *Here's Morgan*. Henry Morgan was the iconoclast of the time—so between Morgan and newspapers such as *The Star* and *The Compass*, they stayed on top of the liberal opinions of the day.

Unfortunately the radio holds a disturbing memory. It was a December Sunday and we were visiting my grandmother's house on East 31st Street. My father was attending a football game between the football Giants and Dodgers. The news came over the radio describing the Japanese attack on Pearl Harbor. I was still quite young. I became very frightened, affected not only by the serious tone of the news announcer but also by the concerned looks on the adult faces huddled around the radio. I was afraid that at any minute the Japanese would be marching down East 31st Street or found hiding under our beds, in the closets, or under a bush in the

backyard. It was a very real, childish fear. When my father got home, he wondered aloud why many of the soldiers attending the football game had been alerted to report back to their bases. It was odd, he noted, that such an announcement was made over the stadium's public address system. When my family explained to him the bad news about the attack, his puzzled look quickly drained away.

Both my parents were college graduates, but my father had the misfortune of graduating from college in 1929, certainly not the most auspicious year to start looking for a job. His plans for law school were further dashed by the onslaught of the Depression, so he entered the silverware business to make his living. Although the family had little means, my early years in Brooklyn were still great fun. The games we played in P.S. 89 included all the street games of the day, including stickball, scully, and marbles. My favorite game was stoopball. I loved playing that game. After throwing a spaldeen against a stoop, a player scored runs based on how far the ball traveled across the street. If you got a "pointer" or a "killer"—hitting the sharp edge of the stoop—the ball traveled very far, and if it hit the house across the street, it was a home run! Lesser traveled shots were scored a triple, a double, or a single. I was the acknowledged master around kids in the street, even though stoopball required very little eye/hand coordination and demanded little concentration. It didn't require

tremendous power, either. When you hit a stoop's point just right, regardless of the speed you threw the ball, a lively spaldeen would just take off. If there was an International Stoopball Championship, I'd have been right up there on top. Sad to say, the level of proficiency I demonstrated in other sports never quite matched my celebrated prowess in stoopball.

On April 12, 1945 (when I was six years

old), I looked out the window and saw my mother crying as she

hung clothes out to dry. I ran out to her and she took me in her

arms, hugged me, and explained that President Franklin Delano

Singer and composer

Roosevelt had died. Although I didn't understand it, I cried, too.

All of Brighton Beach was in mourning that day.... Brighton

Beach was a unique section of Brooklyn. In the 1940s it was a

lower- to middle-class Jewish neighborhood where everyone

looked the same and talked the same, families spoke Yiddish at

home, had no contact with other neighborhoods, and thought the

NEIL
SEDAKA

whole world was Jewish. I wouldn't lay eyes on a WASP for months at a time....

By the time I was ready to begin school, I realized I was different from the other kids. I just didn't fit in with guys like the fat kid who was the neighborhood tough and his sidekick....

Murray Newman of Brighton Beach was my first piano teacher. I was on Book Six of the John Thompson series within six months...I spent so much time practicing, Mom had to bring my meals to the piano. My performances were oohed and aahed over.... By the time I entered P.S. 225 for the seventh and eighth grades, my classmates were asking me to play the piano at every opportunity. During assembly when the film broke down, all the kids would start chanting, "We want Neil." As frightened as I was, I always got up to play....

With my new found confidence [I got playing rock 'n' roll], I started dating girls in 1952. I was having pizza at Andrea's Pizza Parlor with Carole Klein, my girlfriend, who later became Carole King, creator of many rock classics. There was a big flashing Wurlitzer jukebox at Andrea's, and out of it was blasting the strangest and most erotic sound I'd ever heard. It was called "Earth Angel," sung by the Penguins.

"It's got imperfections," I commented to Carole. We were pop-music junkies and analyzed every hit record. "They're singing slightly off-key, but it's an honest reflection of the times we're living in, socially and emo-

tionally, don't you think? Alan Freed calls it rock 'n' roll on his show.

"Whatever it is, it moves my ass," Carole said.

Carole was a scrawny kid with dirty-blond hair, a long nose, and funny buck teeth. She was one of a group of musical teenagers who hung around together, singing on street corners and at sock hops. Doo-wop singing originated in New York City. It was a spinoff from black R&B records. The doo-wop group usually consisted of four or more singers. They would congregate on New York street corners, in school yards, or in some hallway that had a natural echo. The songs they sang almost always had the same four chords, I, VI, II, V, or in the key of C, C major, A minor, D minor, D minor, G major. The group sang a cappella—without instrumentation. The lyrics dealt with young love, and the accents were unmistakably New York.... The bass singers usually had an intricate part, jumping up and down octaves. There was always a high falsetto on top. The harmonies were close, in triad style. There were lots of shoo-bops, sha-la-las, lang-a-langs, shoo-doops, and shoo-be-doos. Carole and I swooned over them. We did a kind of bump-and-grind slow dance to them called the fish. It gave Carole and me a chance to get *very* close to each other. Bodies rubbed. It got sexy and sensuous....

At school one day she said, "Would you mind if some friends and I came over to hear you rehearse sometime?"

"No, not all," I replied. We often had friends drop by. "Why don't you come tonight?" That evening ... we played our hearts out. I loved to perform. When I took a break at the piano, Carole sat down and tried to emulate me, crudely playing my songs with one finger. She had perfect pitch and could harmonize at the drop of a hat.

Carole began coming to every rehearsal, and we began playing musical games together. "Carole," I would ask, "tell me what notes I'm playing." I would press down several keys with both hands. "You have to tell me every note without looking at the piano." Carole would pick out the notes flawlessly. "You're playing F, A flat, A, B flat, B, C, E, and G with the right hand and two perfect fifths, C and G and G and D, with your left." Everyone in the room would gasp and applaud....

Soon Carole and I could recreate every piano fill or musical lick on the original rock 'n' roll recordings. We listened to the radio religiously and knew every song in the Top 40. Within a short while, Carole and I began to attract our own following. When the word got out we were attending a dance, fans chased after us, hoping to see us perform. We were high-school celebrities.

Carole's mother couldn't stand me. Carole was a straight-A student, and her mother felt I was a bad influence on her daughter. Carole started a group called the Cosigns because of me, and we seemed to go everywhere together. One Sunday shortly after we'd started going steady, I asked Carole if she'd like to go mambo dancing in Lakewood, New Jersey. Her mother almost said no. But when I informed Mrs. Klein that my mother and father would be driving and chaperoning, Carole was given permission to go. We picked her up at her family's apartment on Ocean Avenue and Avenue Z in a borrowed car, as we didn't own one. My mother whispered to me as Carole got in, "Couldn't you pick a pretty one?" I whispered back, "Wait till you hear her sing and play the piano. Then tell me what you think."

It was a three-hour drive from Brighton to Lakewood, and Carole and I had the radio constantly blaring rock 'n' roll songs as we sat in the back of the car holding hands and singing lyrics. Our relationship was already much more than musical—for the second time in my life I was in love.

At age sixteen, Carole was already a heavy smoker. During the car ride she constantly lit one cigarette after another. My mother was horrified. Nice girls, she felt, didn't smoke. When we got to the hotel, she took me aside. "Why does she smoke like that? What do you see in her?"

"Mother, leave her alone. She's amazing, and incredibly talented."

Carole and I spent a wonderful day dancing to the mambo band. During the dance breaks we each took turns entertaining the hotel guests at the piano, to their appreciative applause. By evening I wanted desperately to be alone with her. More than

anything else in the world I wanted to touch her, to have her in my arms and kiss her.

Later as we returned to Brooklyn, Carole and I sat in the backseat kissing and petting.

FOR A NICKEL YOU COULD BUY A NATHAN'S FAMOUS ORANGE DRINK, HAMBURGER, ROAST BEEF, POTATO CHIPS AND, OF COURSE, THE BEST TASTING FRANKFURTER ANYWHERE!

Award-winning children's book
illustrator and author

OVERLEAF: VICTORY
CELEBRATION BANNERS
HUNG OVER MANY
BROOKLYN STREETS AFTER
THE END OF WORLD WAR II.

When I was born on the top of the dining-

room table in an apartment in Brooklyn, it was the beginning to

what seemed like an endless procession of family upheavals. In

the days of the early thirties, when landlords were required to

paint a leased apartment, my mother, who had a fanatic aversion

to the smell of paint and the attendant chaos that painting an

apartment caused, would choose instead to move the family to

another apartment. So every three years or thereabouts, we

would move to another neighborhood—Bensonhurst, Bay

Ridge, Flatbush, back to Bensonhurst. We also moved according

MAURICE

SENDAK

to my father's income, upgrading or downgrading to a new address based on the money he earned. This constant moving made it very difficult for me in terms of school and friends. After touring several neighborhoods in Brooklyn, we finally settled into an apartment on 59th Street and 18th Avenue in Bensonhurst.

The most impressionable influences in my young life in Brooklyn were my maternal grandfather and Mickey Mouse. Though I never knew him, I was constantly fascinated and intrigued by my grandfather's photo that hung on the wall in my bedroom. He was a promising rabbi and scholar, whose wife had worked very hard in a ghetto town outside Warsaw to support his studies. The hope his family had for his success vanished the day this handsome, bearded young man suddenly died. His photo became an icon for my family's struggle in Brooklyn, and a memorial for my mother's devoted love. She would stand and admire his photo while recounting her days with him in Poland. But as I was to find out later, the photo represented more than loving memories to her. And it was I who unwittingly brought those feelings to the surface. I was a sickly child and twice came very close to death. During one episode of feverish delirium, I began a long conversation with my grandfather's photo, and at one point sat up from my bed and reached out to touch him. These actions terrified my mother, who feared her father was calling me from eternity. The next morning when I

recovered, I faced a naked wall. The oval rim of dust that surrounded the frame was all that was left. After my mother died many years later, I found the photo in a bottom drawer, torn into many pieces. It took me several years to restore the photograph and today it hangs again in my bedroom. So, in a sense, my grandfather has come back.

The very first time I saw Mickey Mouse, I was totally enthralled. Mickey Mouse was a wonderful character whom I absolutely adored in my youth. I loved sitting in a dark Brooklyn theater watching his antics on the screen. He was a fierce character, a great hero to a generation of children enraptured by the sensational graphics of Walt Disney. Mickey Mouse was to make a lasting impression. Some of the characters I created early in my career began their names with *M*, partly because of Mickey Mouse, some because of my first name, and others because of Mozart and Melville, two of my favorite artists. It seems I've always done well with names that begin with *M*.

Although my father found it difficult to make ends meet during the years after the Depression, the love he had for his children always remained strong. Some of my best memories are the evenings my father would tell bedtime stories to my brother Jack and me. He didn't read us stories because he couldn't read English, so he would spin beautifully imaginative stories, folktales from the old country, and off-beat Bible

yarns. There were some stories that were a little off-color, as I found out later when I repeated them in school. He loved to tease us with cliff hangers. Upon reaching the climax of a fascinating story, he would suddenly click out the light and wish us a good night's sleep. His imagination was wonderfully active. I can vividly recall the night, at his suggestion, I stared out my Brooklyn bedroom window, watching for an angel. I was once again under the siege of a sickness and my father counseled me that to get better I should watch for a passing angel in the sky. He advised, "Don't blink!" Taking him up on his word, I stared outside the window for what seemed like hours. After some time and with my eyes watering, I soon imagined the sight of an angel. I remember calling out to my father from my bed that I saw the angelic sight, and almost immediately he came running into the room.

Contributing to my sickly condition was the stress I found in school. I hated school. My older sister and brother were very intelligent and had done well in their studies, so part of the problem was that I was competing with their achievements. The teachers would never let me forget their accomplishments. Complicating matters was the fact I wrote with my left hand, so they would do terrible things to break me of the habit. I was forced to hold my left hand behind my back and write with my right hand. If I forgot, the teacher would hit me with a ruler. They assigned me to a back-of-the-room seat, where the other left-handers and slow learners sat. If I did well, I was "promoted" to a seat closer to the front. Fueled by the social hierarchy the school created, the smarter kids naturally looked down on the kids in the back. If you were a "back row" kid, you were made to feel inferior. After a while, we identified with our supposed inferiority. Because of the tension in school, I developed stomach cramps and preferred being at home. I was known as the kid who would throw up halfway across the room if I was called upon. After a couple of incidents, it didn't take long for a teacher to learn not to call on Sendak. This feeling of inferiority lasted through high school. When I started to gain recognition for my drawing abilities at Lafayette High School, my self-image finally improved.

Friday nights were especially happy times, because that was the night my mother and father would take me to the movies. Our favorite movies theaters were the Kingsway and the Jewel on Eastern Parkway, where they would show classic movies. I particularly enjoyed fantasy films. *The Invisible Man* and *King Kong* were two of my favorites, and I also loved Laurel and Hardy. While my mother enjoyed the shows, her desire to go to the Friday night movies was fueled mainly by the free dish she received. She got her better dishes from the movie houses, so in a way I profited from my mother's rabid interest in rounding out her Saturday night dinner set.

Bensonhurst at that time was comprised mainly of Italians and Jews. As a child, however, I thought the whole world was Jewish. I figured there were two types of Jews: sad Jews and happy Jews. The sad Jewish people were those similar to my mother and father, while the happy Jews were like my friend Carmine's parents across the street. I couldn't figure out why one group laughed heartily and the other group cried. Why my parents ate boring food called kosher, while Carmine and his happy Jewish parents ate delicious food called macaroni. I adored the happy people, while feeling melancholy for the sad ones. It was an innocent childhood perspective, compounded by the fact everyone looked the same. The mothers were all overweight and they all dressed badly. The fathers were all struggling, all working very hard. But even though happy and sad differences did exist, everyone got along.

Our Victrola was kept in the kitchen,

along with the crystal radio sets that my grandfather built for us.

The kitchen itself kept changing. I was born at home—613 Mid-

wood Street in Brooklyn—on May 26, 1929. My father, Morris

Silverman, was an assistant manager for the Metropolitan Life

Insurance Company, and since he worked on a commission

basis, his income fluctuated wildly. Every once in a while he

would land a very big client like Mr. Schwartz of Chock Full

o'Nuts, who later changed his name to Mr. Black. Each time my

father signed up an important new customer, we would move,

Opera singer

BEVERLY SILLS

189

though never more than a few blocks. Although the apartment where I was born was quite spacious, the first apartment I actually remember was a one-bedroom flat at 580 Empire Boulevard in Brooklyn. I shared the bedroom with my parents. My brothers—Sidney, six years older than I, and Stanley, four years older—slept in a Hide-A-Bed in the foyer. The next apartment I remember, at 948 Lenox Road in Flatbush, was very large and lavish. We didn't stay there long, because I developed seriously inflamed sinuses. The houses there had been built on marsh flats, and it was too damp for me. So we pulled up stakes and moved back to Empire Boulevard. . . .

My father was a strict parent—there was absolutely no give-and-take in our relationship. He laid down the law, and we obeyed. Papa never lectured us, nor did he ever lay a finger on any of us, but he knew how to make a point. He was a demanding man and expected no less of us than he expected of himself. I once scored a ninety-eight on an arithmetic test, and I remember his saying, "I don't like ninety-eights. I only like one hundreds."

We moved to Sea Gate just after I graduated from P.S. 91, which went up to the eighth grade. I was accepted into the High School of Music and Art, then located on Convent Avenue at 135th Street in Manhattan. To get there from Sea Gate, I took a bus, a trolley, the BMT subway up to 42nd Street, and then transferred over to the IRT sub-

way, where I took an express uptown to 125th Street and then transferred to a local, which took me within a few blocks of the school. It took almost three hours to get to Music and Art, which meant that to be on time for my eight o'clock class, I had to leave home at 5 A.M. If I left school promptly at three o'clock, I didn't get home until six, which left no time for singing or piano practice or even homework.

After my first week at Music and Art, Papa and I had a long talk. He thought all that commuting was too much for me, and I agreed. The problem was what to do about it. At the time, *the* school to go to in Brooklyn was Erasmus Hall. It was unlikely I'd be accepted there, however, because we lived way out of the district. My mother nevertheless phoned Mr. Lipschitz, the principal of P.S. 91. She told him about the problem I was having with Music and Art and that I wanted to attend Erasmus Hall. Mr. Lipschitz advised her to send me to Abraham Lincoln High School, which was in our district. Mama insisted that I wanted to go to Erasmus, and that my father had volunteered to drive me there every morning and pick me up every afternoon.

Mr. Lipschitz liked me—I'd been valedictorian of my graduating class—so he wrote a letter to the principal of Erasmus Hall saying that I was an outstanding student, and that as long as my father provided transportation for me, the school should make an exception in my case. Ersmus Hall accepted me on that condition: Papa had to drive me to

A HORSE AND SLEIGH WAS THE
WINTERTIME TRANSPORTATION FOR
MANY FLATBUSH RESIDENTS DURING
THE EARLY 1900s.

school in the morning and pick me up in the afternoon. There simply wasn't any way to get from Sea Gate to Erasmus Hall by public transportation.

I got to know my father very well during those years. Papa had to be in his office at seven-thirty each morning, and my first class didn't start until eight-forty. Every morning he'd drive me to DuBrow's cafeteria, right next door to Erasmus. We'd get there before seven o'clock, and we'd arrive with copies of four morning newspapers—the *Times*, the *Daily Mirror*, the *Daily News*, and the *Herald Tribune*. He'd get a cup of coffee for himself, a half cup for me (I'd fill the rest up with cream), and we'd both feast on hot almond horns. To this day, whenever I see one of those pastries, a wave of nostalgia washes over me.

We'd then sit and read the papers, and Papa would ask me questions about some of the day's new stories. It was a wonderful way to learn what was going on in the world. I felt very close to my father. He'd leave me in Du-Brow's at around seven twenty, and I'd sit there reading the papers until it was time to go to school.

The news then was awful, of course. It was a somber time for the family and for our country. World War II had started. We learned what the Nazis were doing to Jews in Germany and how they were out to conquer Europe and the rest of the world. We knew how important it was for America to win the war.

A lot of neighborhood boys went off to fight in Europe and never returned. My brothers had a friend named Stanley Green-berg, whose father owned the Baltic Linen Company—he always used to say his dad worked in a sheet house. Stanley was killed in the war. So were a lot of other boys we knew. Sea Gate is a residential community of single-family houses, and when I'd walk down the street I'd see many windows displaying the Gold Star.

Comedian

PHIL

When I was eight I sang at a stag coming-

out-of-jail party for a local hoodlum named Little Doggie. In the

middle of my number, a man was shot dead at my feet. The

Brownsville section of Brooklyn was a tough neighborhood in

the 1920s, so I didn't think that was too strange. My first reac-

tion was, is the program chairman going to pay me my three

dollars? My specialty number was "Break the News to Mother," a

surefire tearjerker. My audience—the pugs in Willie Beecher's

gym, where I often sang while they were being rubbed down; the

guys in the beer halls; the Murder Inc. enforcers in the hoodlum

SILVERS

clubs—always wiped away a furtive tear....

It was Little Doggie's special request. He was not a lovable figure in the neighborhood, but he came by his name honestly. A fellow hoodlum had a stranglehold on him in a street brawl, so Doggie raised himself on his hands and bit off the guy's thumb.

Little Doggie's coming-out party followed a routine scenario. Friends paid for the hall and drinks. It was stag, but very proper. No girls, just Prohibition booze and welcome back, buddy. Guns were checked at the door. The guest of honor was responsible for the peace of the evening, and any undue violence was a great affront to him. I never told Mama about this. She never asked, "Was a bum shot at the party?" so I never brought it up.

I was two kinds of a kid. I didn't mind being alone but I also flourished in the company of others. I was bored silly at school. I was the youngest in my family, so my five brothers and two sisters didn't have time for me. And since my parents were immigrants, I didn't have much to talk about with them. The only way I could get together with people was by singing. Anywhere. Anytime. So I started very early....

We didn't own bicycles, read comic books, or smoke marijuana; the only pills we popped were Smith Brothers licorice flavor. In those days you did two things on the street: you went looking for a fight, or you stole.

Sometimes both.

Brownsville was Jewish turf. No anti-Semitism here. A strange face in the neighborhood had to say "bread and butter" in Yiddish fast to keep from being mangled. The Irish kids acquired remarkable Yiddish accents.... The most respected residents were the gangsters. Abe Reles recruited his executioners for Murder Inc. here. They'd kill or maim anybody for a reasonable fixed price. The Amberg boys, Pretty Boy and Hymie, were vicious outlaws—they didn't even respect the code of the underworld. They were crazy. At a restaurant table, using the prongs of his dinner fork, Pretty Boy mangled the face of his friend for accidently stepping on his newly shined shoes. And then there was Benny Siegel. Nobody ever called him Bugsy to his face. *Nobody*. I met Benny in Hollywood years later and developed a strange admiration for this gangster. These were our heroes. They had rolls of bills in their pockets, and nobody dared slug them.

I started my street career modestly enough. The city was building Thomas Jefferson High School across the street from my home, on the vacant lot we used for baseball. They had a hell of a nerve. We climbed the fence at night and pulled out the water pipes; the water would run down and soften the cement. Floors collapsed. Then we'd sell the pipe. We delayed the construction for six months....

As for street fighting, my heart wasn't in it. Gang fights against other neighborhoods were compulsory. I had to be in there swinging, and sometimes I hit somebody. But the blood . . . it upset my stomach....

My best secret weapon was my mouth. I could always improvise a way out. I recall an argument with a tough little egg who was called Chinzo because of his protruding chin. I fractured my thumb on that chin. My roundhouse swing only made him laugh, and I knew I was doomed. I looked up to our apartment window: "Isn't that my mother calling me? Yeah, Mom. I'm coming right up." At nine I already had a bit of Bilko in me.

Mama signed me up for Hebrew school, to salvage me from the "bad bums on the corner." The gnarled old rabbi, in the prescribed gray beard and black gabardine, gave private lessons in his black cellar tenement. He taught Hebrew by rote, and the mumbo jumbo of the rituals made no sense to me. By the second session I hated Hebrew and I hated the old man. He'd slap my palm with a ruler when I refused to recite. One afternoon I pushed him back into his chair as he came at me with the ruler. That was *chutzpah* to push a *rav!* He unbuckled his strap; I ran out and never came back. For a long time the rabbi said nothing to my mother because he was paid by the week.

The time I saved as a Hebrew dropout was spent at the Supreme Theater, a neighborhood movie house where Gladys, an older women (she must have been twenty-four), accompanied the silent films on a wheezy organ.

I always sat behind Gladys, fascinated by her impetuous manipulation of the keys and pedals. One night the reel broke in the middle of *Way Down East*. The projectionist flashed a slide: A MOMENT PLEASE. It took forever to patch that film; the audience hooted and stamped on the floor. I jumped up on my seat and began to sing. Nobody asked me— it just seemed to be the right thing to do. Gladys, astonished, came in a couple bars later on "Big Boy," a very peppy number.... A smash. They wouldn't let me go, even after the movie began. And so I was launched on a new career. I'd sit there every night, and whenever a reel broke, I'd leap up on the stage with "Big Boy" and other novelties. What a flow of power. A big audience—not a family. *Strangers!* And they applauded me. I wasn't paid a nickel, but I got into the Supreme *free*. I was the envy of the neighborhood. I was known as the reel-breaker-down singer.

Actor

I'm a diehard Brooklynite. A friend of

mine tells me that the best way for someone to get my attention is

to say he's from Brooklyn. I was, and still am, enchanted with

the place. It's a beautiful borough with lots of character and a

diversity of people unmatched anywhere else. When I think of

Brooklyn, I think of soda-fountain egg creams, two hamburgers

for a quarter, my P.S. 213 sixth-grade schoolteacher, Mrs. Ar-

vins, who everyone had a crush on, including me, and my adoles-

cent dream of being an astronomer. My family moved around

quite a bit when I was young. We first moved to the Brownsville

FOLLOWING PAGE: THE WILLIAMSBURGH SAVINGS BANK CLOCK WAS FIRST ILLUMINATED ON DECEMBER 24, 1928. THE CLOCK WEIGHS 900 POUNDS AND THE DIAL MEASURES 27 FEET ACROSS. EACH HOUR MARKER IS 52 INCHES LONG.

JIMMY SMITS

section and then to the Bronx and then left for a two-year stay in Puerto Rico. When we returned to the States, we moved to Vermont Street in the East New York section of Brooklyn. I spent my teenage years in East New York and my early adulthood in Flatbush on Ocean Avenue between J and K. One of my fondest memories of living in Brooklyn was playing football for Thomas Jefferson High School under Moe Finkelstein. Moe was quite a character. He was a strict disciplinarian, who worked his team very hard, but at the same time you could sense he really loved working with young people. I started my football career on the sandlots of Brooklyn and eventually made the Jefferson varsity squad as an outside linebacker. The team always looked forward to the preseason summer camp, when Moe would take the whole squad away into the hills of Pennsylvania. That week was always great fun, especially since we shared the camp with the team from New Utrecht High School. I remember one year, as we were heading out to Pennsylvania, we passed Shea Stadium. I always sat near Moe on our bus trips. Just as Shea came into view, he turned to me and said: "Jim, you could be playing there someday." Things, of course, didn't work out that way, but Moe was great at making you believe that you could do just about anything.

One of the toughest decisions I made in high school was quitting the football team to join the Jefferson drama club. Besides

giving up the team jacket, I could no longer sit with the team in the cafeteria. Worse, I feared what my ex-teammates would think of me. What motivated the change was my drama experience at George Gershwin Junior High School. Gershwin's two music teachers, Rhoda Pollack and Robert Newton, produced an annual musical production. These lavish musicals were a tradition in Gershwin for many years. Ms. Pollack was in charge of the singing while Mr. Newton coordinated the music, and if you were selected for a part, you were looked upon as somebody special in school. I always landed a role in these musicals and immediately fell in love with acting. So, although I was enjoying football, the urge to act still lingered in the back of my mind. When I made the decision to join the drama club, football had to be dropped. There just wasn't enough time to do both. On opening night of my first Jefferson production—we performed *Purlie Victorious*—the whole football squad came to watch me perform. When the curtain came down at the end of the evening, the guys gave me a standing ovation. They recognized that acting was what I really wanted to do, and they enthusiastically supported my decision.

Chinese handball, pick-up basketball games, fishing off the pier in Rockaway, and singing on street corners were big parts of my Brooklyn reality in East New York. When we wanted to get out of the neighborhood, the big attraction was the St. George Hotel pool in downtown Brooklyn. The

hotel was sumptuously decorated in Art Deco, and I remember marveling at its interior. As we got older we attended the dances that were held there. East New York was a neighborhood filled with many struggling, poor families, some surviving and others failing. One guy the whole neighborhood looked up to was Junior, the owner of the corner *bodega*. He had taken a run-down, rinky-dink store and transformed it into a successful business. He was a terrific person who would extend credit to people who didn't have money, give free candy to little children, or let us older kids wash his windows for pocket change. A hard-working fellow who worked sixteen-hour days, he was not afraid to protect what was his. I remember one night, as my friends and I stood on the corner of Vermont and Riverdale outside his store, we watched as he pulled out a shotgun to thwart a couple of robbers. Everyone respected Junior and the business he built up, which made him enough money to buy a house and move his family back to Puerto Rico.

My home was typical of that of the families living in East New York. We were struggling to get ahead. My father was very strict guy who came from Surinam and my mother was of Puerto Rican ancestry. The family consisted of me and my two younger sisters. Friday night was the family night out and it was a big deal to go to the McDonald's on Pennsylvania Avenue or the local Chinese restaurant for dinner. One year all the kids in the neighborhood bought leather jackets, and I re-

member asking my parents for a jacket, too. When they explained they couldn't afford to buy me a new one, I went to a pawn shop near the Brooklyn Academy of Music and bought a used leather jacket there. Because my mother was religious, we were all expected to go to church on Sundays. Easter Sunday was the really big family day. It was a yearly ritual to go to Coney Island with the family and strut your new clothes on the board-walk. Another big event was the obligatory visit to the A&S Christmas window on Fulton Street. The Manhattan guys had Macy's and us Brooklyn kids had A&S.

When I look back on Brooklyn, I think of the neighborhoods there. To me, that's what Brooklyn's all about. It personifies, in a very positive way, the true definition of the word "neighborhood." People are affectionate about Brooklyn because of the people who live there, its history, and its character. It's the real world. During the bicentennial celebration, I remember standing on the Brooklyn Promenade, among the crowd who came from various neighborhoods to watch the celebration in the New York harbor. I was struck by the number and various types of people who stood on the Promenade that evening. Equally moving was the harmony and the good feeling everyone felt for each other. It was a sight to behold. I doubt the folks across the river were having as good a time that night as us Brooklynites.

D U K E

The Brooklyn Dodgers'
"Duke of Flatbush"

When I saw Ebbets Field for the first time

as a Brooklyn Dodger, it was love at first sight. I loved that old

ball park and everything about it, and that covered a lot. There

was Hilda Chester with her cowbell in the outfield stands, bellow-

ing out with leather lungs, "Hilda's here!" There was a fan

named Eddie Barton who used to blow a tin whistle. The Sym-

Phony band strolled through the stands playing Dixieland mu-

sic, and from his seat Jack Pierce sent up balloons with Cookie

Lavagetto's name on them, because Cookie was his favorite

player. Before the game *Happy Felton's Knothole Gang*, a TV

S N I D E R

show where kids got to meet the Dodger players, went on the air from the bullpen.

Tex Rickhart, a film distributor who doubled as the public-address announcer, was another resident character. He'd sit on a chair next to our dugout on the first-base side and announce that "a little boy has been found lost." Or he'd ask, "Will the fans in the front row along the railing please remove their clothes?"

We played with only three umpires in those days, and the five fans in the Sym-Phony would strike up "Three Blind Mice" when a call went against us. An opposing player walking back to the dugout after making an out was accompanied by the tune "The Worms Crawl In, the Worms Crawl Out." As soon as his rear end touched the bench, the Sym-Phony's drummer hit his drum and cymbal. Occasion-

ally an opposing player with a sense of humor would try to fake out the drummer and almost sit down, then bolt up and head for another spot on the bench, but the drummer never allowed himself to be fooled. When the player finally sat down, he always got the treatment. If a player went to the water fountain, the Sym-Phony played "How Dry I Am."

Ebbets Field was the smallest park in the league with only 32,000 seats. A sign said no more than 33,000, including people in the aisles, were permitted, but I think we broke that rule every time the Giants came to Brooklyn. Late in the 1947 season they squeezed 37,512 fans into the old park—for a Giants game.

The outfield fence had all sorts of advertising on it, something you don't see in today's new parks. The Ebbets Field

fence was a who's who of merchants and products—Griffin Microsheen Shoe Polish, the Brass Rail Restaurant, Van Heusen Shirts, Gem Razor Blades, and the sign that everybody remembers: HIT SIGN, WIN SUIT. It advertised a clothing store owned by a guy named Abe Stark—and was at the bottom of the fence below the scorecard, right behind Carl Furillo. Because it was at the base of the fence, 330 feet from home plate, and with the Skoonj right in front of it, very few hitters were going to hit that sign on the fly. Abe Stark only lost about five suits, and he once gave Skoonj a suit for protecting the sign so well. There are those who say the name recognition Abe Stark got from the sign over the years was a big factor when he was elected Borough President of Brooklyn years later.

The fans weren't the only

characters there. The Dodgers had two of their own, our batboy, "Charley the Brow," and our clubhouse attendant, John Griffin. The Brow, a man in his twenties like most of us, got his name from his thick, dark, bushy eyebrows. He was a man to be reckoned with. In addition to being an efficient batboy, he had influence in other important pursuits. He could get you a ride home, solve various problems for

you, and sign your autograph better than you could. Sometimes the Brow would sign the team balls for us. I don't want to disillusion any fans who might have baseballs autographed by the Dodger team in those years, but the Brow signed a lot of them—for all twenty-five players, the coaches, and the manager. He could help you out of almost any jam, and he had some "boys" to do what he told them. One night three young men were really getting on me from the center-field bleachers, and after a while I'd had enough. The next time I was in the on-deck circle, with the Brow kneeling next to me the way the batboy always does, I said, "Hey, Brow—you got your boys here tonight?"

He says, "Sure, Duke, You need something done?"

I said, "Yeah. See those three guys in the bleachers, in the upper deck?" I nodded in their direction, being careful not to point.

"Yeah. Why?"

"They've been riding me pretty hard all night and now they're beginning to question my ancestry."

The Brow says, "You want me to do something about it?"

"Yeah. Send your boys up there and see if they can quiet them down, will you?"

The next inning, while I was sitting in the dugout, I looked out at that spot in the bleachers. The three guys were gone. I never found out what the Brow had his boys do, and I never asked.

John Griffin was just as

much a character. He was big and heavy, smoked cigars, and had an endless collection of crazy hats and costumes and disguises. He'd be dressed as a monk one game, a baby the next, with a sheet for a diaper and wearing a baby bonnet. It was always anybody's guess what he would be for the next game. We called him the Senator. He kept us entertained while performing the almost impossible job of keeping our equipment straight, making sure it was in the right city at the right time, and doing everything else an equipment manager, or clubhouse boy, has to do. John was the one who gave me the number 4. When I was a rookie in 1947 at Ebbets Field, just before the season started, he told me some of the uniform numbers he had available. I asked him about number 4. "I haven't given that to anybody since Dolf Camilli," he said. I knew why. Camilli was a Dodger favorite from the 1930s and early 1940s, a home-run-hitting first basemen, and Griffin obviously felt some sentiment and loyalty about his number. He gave it to me anyhow, reminding me that Camilli was a long-ball hitter, so John would be expecting me to hit a lot of home runs too.

I was thrilled to get the number of my favorite baseball player of all time, then and now, and he wasn't a Dodger, he was a Yankee—Lou Gehrig.... Getting to wear Lou Gehrig's number and play for the Brooklyn Dodgers was as much as a twenty-year-old ex-sailor right out of the Navy and up from the Texas League could dare ask for.

Abstract-realist painter

The trolley car trip to Prospect Park is one of my finest memories during my early days in Brooklyn. I was born in Memorial Hospital in 1920 and lived on Bergen Street for the first seven years of my life. Saturdays and Sundays were days spent with my parents, and I remember enjoying our daily excursions to Prospect Park via the trolley line. Although I was enrolled in elementary school in Brooklyn, I was soon uprooted to Bellport, Long Island, part of the Brookhaven Township, an area where my ancestry dates back to 1655. After graduating from college, and living for several years in Manhat-

GEORGE TOOKER

tan, I returned to Brooklyn in 1953.

I was looking for space to live and work, so a friend and I

it. The person at the Buildings Department feebly explained the porch was a fire hazard, yet our argument, that no other wooden

and elderly people. In fact, many of the brownstones were fairly worn down and quite a few were empty. Yet despite the advancing

brought a lovely old house on State Street in Brooklyn Heights for $12,500. The house was the perfect solution for our needs, although problems immediately arose when we applied for the certificate of occupancy. The building was a former rooming house and we wanted to transform it into a two-family. After our application was reviewed, we were ordered by the Buildings Department to dismantle the glass-walled, wooden porch in back of the house. Judging from the design and style of the woodwork, the porch was built around 1840, the same time as the house. Why then it was allowed previously, when the building was a rooming house, as opposed to why it now had to go, wasn't spelled out to us. Clearly there was no sound reason to destroy

structure existed near the house, went unheeded. The Buildings Department official was adamant. We had to agree to dismantle part of the house, or our application would be rejected. For us to get a mortgage, we needed the certificate of occupancy, so we reluctantly agreed to dismantle the porch and hired an architect to supervise the work. The episode was not without its merits. It proved to be an inspiration. Soon thereafter, spurred by the frustration of fighting "City Hall," I painted *Government Bureau*.

Brooklyn Heights in the early fifties, in the pregentry days, was a lovely area complete with rooming houses and very pleasant neighbors. Much of the neighborhood was comprised of friendly Puerto Rican families

age of the neighborhood, there was a feeling of space on the streets, even during the summer days when the rooming-house tenants sat outside on their stoops, looking for some relief from the summer's heat. The streets had a very relaxed, cordial atmosphere. Although there were several artists in the area, the neighborhood wasn't especially an enclave for artists back then, as it grew to be in later years. I painted in my State Street studio for seven years. In 1960, tired of being landlords and growing weary of the onslaught of a new generation moving into the neighborhood, we sold the house and moved away.

Dancer and singer

Sundays for the Vereen family meant at-

tending church services and singing gospel music praising the

Lord. Like many women who attended the Unity Baptist Church

in Bedford-Stuyvesant, my mother was an ardent gospel singer,

as was Mrs. Mary Eddy, my godmother. Mother Mary was known

for rousing up a Sunday congregation, and I've always credited

her as the very first person who taught me how to work an

audience. As I grew older and began to sing in the church choir,

she would put me through the paces and instruct me on the fine

art of performing. Taking me by the hand as she made her way

BEN
VEREEN

down the church's main aisle, she'd explain the differences between singing and performing in front of the morning assembly. Attracted to the adulation of any audience when I was a kid, I immediately got hooked on entertaining.

Creative energy perpetually filled the streets of Bedford-Stuyvesant. Down the block from our apartment on Chauncey Street was a shoeshine parlor owned by a couple of lively vaudevillians. Their names were Tip and Tap. The place always buzzed with activity, especially on Sunday mornings when the neighborhood men came to get their shoes shined before services. Tip and Tap choreographed a wonderful routine as they shined a man's shoes, snapping shine rags, clicking shoe brushes, spinning and tapping with their dance shoes. Because they didn't allow kids in the store, we stood outside and sneaked peeks through the window, imitating their steps as they performed. We never understood why they'd never let us in. Later, we found out that a shoeshine and a dance routine weren't the only reasons the parlor was so popular. It was also the favorite place to go for a quick shot of whiskey.

While my father worked in a paint factory during the day, my mom labored night shifts as a maintenance woman. Although her hours were long and brutal, I was particular excited when she got a job working at the Loews King Theater. Many nights I accompanied my mom to work, and after everyone cleared out, she'd

ONE OF THE MAJOR THOROUGHFARES OF BROOKLYN IS FLATBUSH AVENUE, HOME TO THE BROOKLYN PARAMOUNT, SEEN ON THE RIGHT.

205

begin her cleaning. For me, it was stage time! I'd run down the aisle, jump on the stage, and perform little dance routines for her as she cleaned. My dance steps were all improvised, and I'd imagine all those empty seats filled with people. I loved those evenings. By the end of her shift I was all tuckered out, and she'd have to scrape me off a back-row theater seat, where I usually had fallen asleep.

To nurture my desire to perform, my mom enrolled me in the Star Time Dance Studio on Utica Avenue. Almost immediately I knew this place wasn't for me. It was too restrictive, there were too many kids in the class and I wasn't allowed to freely express myself. My mother then registered me in the Dale Green Dance Studio on Flatbush Avenue. I spent three wonderful years there, from the time I was ten through the beginning of my days in high school. I had a great time at that studio. Dale Green sponsored in-studio recitals and produced amateur shows in hospitals or homes. Most times I was given free rein on what I could dance. Dale Green's daughter and I were the big stars at the studio, and we'd improvise and create movements from jazz dancing to free form. It was a wonderful opportunity, and I'm forever indebted to my mother for all the hours she sacrificed taking me to Saturday morning studio lessons, recitals, and dance productions.

I was attending P.S. 178 while performing at Dale Green, and though I was an average student, I was building a reputation on my performances in school productions and my achievements in track and field. Though I enjoyed dancing, my big ambition was to attend Boys High School and become a track-and-field star. During the last year of junior high, however, the school sponsored a production of *The Kind and I*. Although it was a junior-high-school performance, the production was quite lavish, complete with full orchestra, elaborate sets, wonderful costumes, and staged at the best theater in the borough, the Brooklyn Academy of Music. Even though I had never been to a Broadway production, I knew this was a class act. I was given the role of the interpreter. After sitting through the performance of the play, Benjamin Raskin, the principal of P.S. 178, convinced me I'd be wasting my talents at Boys High School and advised me to attend the High School of Performing Arts in Manhattan. I knew nothing about this high school. I didn't know it even existed, but once I got there, I was really turned on. Benjamin Raskin's vision of what I could accomplish literally paved my way for the future.

While attending Performing Arts, I hooked up with Ronald Banks, a fellow from the neighborhood who was a vocalist, piano player, and guitarist. We formed a band called the Sensational Twilights of Brooklyn, and I sang lead with a couple of other singers. We'd play parties and socials and have a grand time. Of course, I still continued to sing with Mary Eddy and her husband, an itinerant preacher who would visit different churches or homes to conduct services. Many Friday evenings and Saturday or Sunday mornings were spent with Mother Mary and Reverend Eddy singing gospel music around Brooklyn.

When I wasn't performing with Ronald Banks or Mother Mary, I spent my free time at the theaters in Brooklyn. The Bedord, the Fox, the Paramount, and the Apollo were my favorite places to check out singing and dance acts like Little Anthony and the Imperials, Bo Diddley, and the Shirelles. These stars always gave exciting performances. I watched their technique, and analyzed how they performed for the audience. The crowds were naturally responsive and always passionate for the music. The fans' enthusiasm was a natural derivative of the energy that was flowing in Brooklyn. It was a great place to be. There were exciting things happening all the time.

Actor

I grew up in the back of a store in the Red

Hook section of Brooklyn during the 1920s. My parents were

running their candy-store business right in the middle of

Brooklyn's Little Italy section at 166 Union Street. We were one

of a handful of Jewish families living in the area. Bertha's Candy

Store, which was named after my mother, was the center for all

the activity going on in Red Hook, from the place to purchase

the daily newspaper, a pack of cigarettes, or some penny candy,

to serving as the message center for the local gangsters. My

father, along with several other shopkeepers on the block, was a

ELI
WALLACH

hindrance in getting parts in their productions. But I wasn't alone. There was another student named Cronkite who was also shut out because of *his* Missouri accent.

The summers between the years I was studying for my master's at the City College of New York, I got a job working for the New York City Parks Department. For whatever reason, the Parks Department wanted to chart the flow of people traffic on Coney Island Beach. Outfitted in my official Parks Department uniform, replete with a shiny badge, I was given a clipboard of questions and told to go around the beach and ask beachgoers things like: "What time do you get here?" "How many times do you leave the beach?" "When did you return?" Not exactly stimulating, thought-provoking or intrusive questions, but nevertheless ones that were met with resistance from the tough Brooklyn crowd. Many times, as I approached a party of beachcombers or began my opening explanation, I'd get cut off with responses like "Who wants to know?" "We didn't do anything!" "That's not my garbage!" "Why, are you giving me a ticket?" That Coney Island beach was a tough house to play.

After finishing up at Texas and attaining a master's in education at CCNY, I was braced to take the teacher's test. Although my schooling was in education, my heart was still in acting. The day I learned I failed the test, I was very relieved. I remember saying to myself, "Thank God! Somebody up there really likes me!" Failing the test was a signal to my family to leave me alone. I immediately got a scholarship to the Neighborhood Playhouse and began chasing my acting dream.

TOP HATS, STARCHED COLLARS AND BONNETS WERE THE DRESS OF THE DAY DURING THE EARLY 1900S IN BROOKLYN, ESPECIALLY IF YOU WERE TO BE PHOTOGRAPHED UNDERNEATH AN ORNAMENTAL URN IN PROSPECT PARK.

M A E

Actress

The Brooklyn I was born in, near the end

of the nineteenth century, was still a city of churches, with their

great bronze bells walloping to the faithful from early dawn, and

a city of waterfront dives where the old forest of the spars of

sailing ships was rapidly being replaced by funnels and the Sands

Street Navy Yard already had a reputation for girl chasers. Gen-

tlemen, and deer, ran wild in Prospect Park. I was born into a

world of much more sunlight and less smoke than now, a world of

ringing horse cars, ragtime music, cakewalks, and Floradora

Sextets, and a sense that the coming new century would be the

W E S T

biggest and the best. The final score is not yet in, but I think this one will make it among the centuries to treasure.

Brooklyn was a city of neat horse-plagued, tree-lined streets, connected by a brand new bridge to Manhattan. Men of affairs, business and otherwise, still drove a pair of horses in a fancy rig, and while beards were still in fashion, the well dressed man-about-town was already waxing the end of his English Guardsman's mustaches and learning to point them with a twist of his ruby-cuff-linked wrist.

There were Brooklyn picnics in the many groves of oak and elm that still existed, and the great iron-wheeled beer drays pulled by four to six large-rumped horses in their polished harnesses were a sight to cheer. There was a fine theater audience—high and low. Girls in tights, and girls without them, and the ragtime beat and the first stirrings of jazz from faraway Storyville were already coming out of the places soon to use Mr. Edison's new electric-light signs. The sports were beginning to appear in the first of the horseless carriages. The lobster palaces, high-button shoes, popular hook-and-ladder fire companies were the things that gave a man standing in the community. I was a child of the new century just around the corner, and I ran toward it boldly.

I was born on a respectable street in Brooklyn on August 17, 1893. I am of English, Irish, and German extraction, which means the usual European intermixture of many unknown genes that keep people lively.

My father, John West, was of English and Irish descent, a tough chip-on-the-shoulder lover of fun and fights. His father was also a John West who came from a long line of John Wests originally from Long Grendon, Buckinghamshire, England. The first John West in America came over in the 1700s.

My father's mother, Mary Jane Copley, was Irish and came to this country at an early age. She was related to the well-known Copleys of Boston and Pittsburgh.

Unlike his brothers, who went through college, my father, a wild laughing man, preferred a life of banging physical action. When he married my mother he was known as "Battling Jack West, Champion of Brooklyn, New York."

My father was an epic figure in Brooklyn. I remember all the stories about him: the gay time when he was courting my mother, and had taken her to a social club outing. He had resented the attentions a club member paid her. A fight started and my father, all knobby with muscles, knocked the rival out with one punch. The club members, a hundred angry men, ganged up on him. Father, in a savage rage, knocked two glass beer mugs together and with the jagged remains cut and slashed his way through the fray, leaving a bloody mob....

Father established a livery stable business of carriages, surreys, and coaches for hire, and maintained horse stands for business or pleasure during the summer at beach resorts. In the winter he also had horse-drawn sleighs, complete with jingle bells.

It was a prosperous business until automobiles became popular, after which time my father became a private detective and established a detective agency. He developed a night alarm system for the protection of stores and warehouses, which were being frequently burglarized by thieves whom the police force could not catch. Later he went into real estate....

Personality is what you as an individual radiate. It's a combination of your thoughts and the way you express them. A person with a great personality never has to act, he just does what he feels. All the training you may get will simply teach you how to express what you feel.

It's love, too—love and respect for yourself, first, then logically for others.

All my concentration on personality and my efforts to develop it got put to a test when I was seven years old, going on eight, and went to "Professor" Watts's dancing school on Fulton Street.... In those days they called any man who was a cardsharp, or a teacher of anything, "Professor."

After two weeks at his studio I had impressed him enough for him to put me on at a Sunday concert at the Royal Theater, which was also on Fulton Street in Brooklyn. This theater played vaudeville shows, but on this Sunday night it was sold out to the Elks, who put on their own show consisting of amateur talent and relatives in addition to the regular vaudeville acts. It was a large theater with two balconies and boxes, and had a twelve-piece orchestra. It was there I made my debut, on my first real stage, and I loved it. It was my first romance.

I was terribly excited about the chance to show my little dances and songs in a big theater, with a big orchestra, big stage, big audience—and best of all to me, a big spotlight. The rest of America could ask for life, liberty, and the pursuit of happiness; I'd take the spotlight. I saw it used in the vaudeville acts that preceded me. I simply had to have it on me. At the proper church affairs and socials where I had entertained they'd never had such a thing. I went to the stage manager. "I have to have a spotlight."

"All right, you'll get one."

I told him at least ten times, even though he agreed each time that I'd get it. I had to be sure. (All my life, casual appearing as I am, I've always double-checked and triple-checked everything.)

Mother was backstage with me, rather worried as to how I would do, this being my first time in a big theater with a large orchestra. "You've only sung and danced to a piano, or with no piano."

I said, "You're more nervous than I am."

I was thrilled and anxious to get out there on that stage—in a spotlight. Who had time to feel upset or nervous? All I was thinking about was what I was going to do when I got out there....

I stepped out on the stage, looked up angrily at the spotlight man in the balcony, stamping my foot. "*Where* is *my* spotlight!" I stamped again and the spotlight moved across stage onto me and caught me in the act of demanding my light. The audience saw me and laughed and applauded. The angry expression on my little face as I impudently stared up at the spotlight man, my exasperated stamping of dancing shoes, explained my delayed entrance. Anyway, they seemed to think my song and my little tiptoeing

dance was cute.... With the spotlight on my shoulders like white mink, I went to center stage and sang my song, "Moving' Day." I did my skirt dance without missing a word or a step. Instead of having stagefright, I was innocently brazen. My angry mood overcame any nervous doubts I might normally have felt. I've never had stagefright in my life.

I was a hit with the audience. They were fine in their applause. I received a gold medal from the [Brooklyn] Elks organization. Papa was proud.

WHILE THE "GOOD OLD DAYS" ARE DELIGHTFUL MEMORIES TODAY, WE TEND TO FORGET THE INCONVENIENCES OF THE PAST. IN MANY OF THE TENEMENTS OF YESTERYEAR UNHEATED OUTHOUSES WERE THE NORM.

L E N N Y

Not many people from the Bedford-

Stuyvesant area of Brooklyn get to go to Yale or Harvard. Re-

Head basketball coach of the
Cleveland Cavaliers

form school would be more in order. The reason is that it's a

ghetto. The people are poor, the kids are rough, and trouble is a

constant companion. But if that's where you were born and that's

all you know from the beginning, either you lick it or it licks

you. I was born there on October 28, 1937, and christened

Leonard Randolph Wilkens, Jr. I don't want to hold myself up as

a shining example. But, then, maybe I should if it will give some

other kids encouragement and faith that they *can* do something

W I L K E N S

constructive with their lives. Throw in the willingness to study and work hard for what you want and anything is possible. I know.

Ask yourself who you are. What do you stand for? You are what you think you are and can become whatever you decide to become. One uses whatever means he can to help himself achieve his goals. Basketball has been my stepping-stone. It has helped me find out who I am, where I am going. As a young-ster, basketball provided me with a way to vent the anger and de-spair that came from being poor, black, and living in the ghetto. A man must act like himself, ac-cording to the reality as he sees himself. If he does not expand himself, then he cannot rise above his present reality.

Maybe, to a certain extent, I was lucky, even though my father died when I was not quite three years old, for I had a strict mother who loved me and my two brothers and two sisters very much. And, in my formative years, when I was about nine, Father Thomas Mannion came to our parish and took me under his wing.

We were as poor as the proverbial church mice and life was exceedingly hard for my mother, Henrietta, a little woman with brownish-blond hair who was a devout Catholic of Irish descent. Her maiden name was Cross and her father's people were from County Cork. Mother worked in a candy factory, did housecleaning, and collected Aid for Dependent Children, yet we still were just barely able to survive.

Christmas is supposed to be a time of toys and sugarplums. I look back on the Christmas days of childhood with mixed emo-tions. Toys? We received clothing. And each year, year in and year out, I was given a pair of roller skates with a certain amount of repugnance. Each night as my mother prayed to God to protect us, to help her make ends meet, and to take care of us, I ached inside with com-passion, offering up my own prayers that I might earn money to help her and make life a little easier. And often, so difficult were our times, I wondered if God was listening. As events de-veloped through the years, I know now that he was.

And much of this credit must go to Father Mannion, who always has appeared larger to me than his five feet, ten inches. A blue-eyed, reddish-haired man, with a grip of steel, his con-fidence has a way of rubbing off on you and making you feel that anything you really desire is at-tainable if you're willing to work for it.

It was my mother and Father Mannion who kept me from straying into trouble. Nor was trouble difficult to find in the Bedford-Stuyvesant section. Kids are always looking for excit-ement. The suggestion was always there, made by one or another. "Let's grab a car somewhere and take a ride." "What can we swipe to raise some dough?" "Let's move in on those other guys' territory and have a rumble."

I've been lined up against a wall with a bunch of others and frisked for weapons by the po-lice. I'm not passing myself off as a saint, but all they found on me were rosary beads. I just hap-pened to have them in my pocket.

You didn't have to look sus-picious to be stopped. It was what the police called preventive action, for every area had its gang, and if you didn't belong to a gang you had extra problems. Most kids joined gangs simply in self-protection. And the "gang wars" were part of my growing-up atmosphere.

I never did join a gang, which meant that I had to be ready to run at a moment's notice. Our neighborhood was integrated. Across the street from our house was a German delicatessen. A few doors down was a Jewish grocery store. I worked for a time in a Greek su-permarket. Our neighbors included a Spanish family.

Water seeks its own level. So do people. Thus, instead of join-ing a gang I associated with boys who were interested in sports and we formed an athletic club that we grandiosely called "The Aristocrats." I guess you'd call us black by national standards, but most of us were of mixed origins. One was part Indian, another part white, and so on. . . .

Joe Mullaney, the Provi-dence basketball coach, came to New York to interview me and check me out with Boys High coach Mickey Fisher and others. I was invited to spend a weekend at Providence and I liked it be-cause it was small and friendly.

Mullaney gave me no absolute commitment but I had a feeling I had been accepted.

June came around and I still hadn't heard from the Providence registrar. A twenty-five-dollar room deposit for my freshman year was due and I didn't have the money, but I finally received notification that my scholarship had been approved. Yet now still another problem developed.

Our family was on welfare and it was the practice that when a boy passed seventeen or graduated from high school he had to go to work to remove his family from the welfare rolls. Having graduated, and as I would be reaching my eighteenth birthday in October 1956 after classes started at Providence, we were advised that I would have to go to work to help support my mother as well as a brother and sister who still were in high school. Again Father Mannion came to the rescue.

He took up our case with the welfare investigator and told him of my college potential. The man, a Mr. Walker, visited our home and discussed the situation with me. He liked what he saw.

"Lenny," he said, "I'm going to stick my neck out for you. The only sensible thing is for you to attend college so that you can be a positive factor in the future of your family. You go on and go to college and we'll see that your family continues to get the welfare help it needs."

I hope he realizes how much he did for us and how greatly I appreciate his help and understanding. Thus the final hurdle was cleared in the realization of a dream.

STOCKING FIREWOOD FROM RAZED SHACKS IN THE SUMMER WAS ONE WAY TO STAY WARM DURING THE COLD MONTHS OF THE WINTER. SEVERAL CHILDREN COLLECT WOOD ON AN EMPTY LOT ON HENRY STREET.

Comedian

I have no idea why my father decided to

leave London. Maybe the cap and hat business got so bad he was

afraid that instead of selling hats, he'd be passing one.... We

lived in Brooklyn because that's where Aunt Marie and Uncle

Morris lived. Uncle Morris was doing all right. And when Aunt

Marie married him, she didn't do badly either. Naturally my

mother and Marie were very close. But not as close as Uncle

Morris. At that time Brooklyn was called "the bedroom of Man-

hattan." People used to say they built the subway under the East

River so those who lived in Brooklyn could sneak home without

HENNY
YOUNGMAN

being seen. But it had a lot of beautiful neighborhoods with large homes in lots of land. To a kid from the slums of London it was like a new world. I used to just walk around looking at the big houses and the wide green lawns. And I hated the whole scene. Because I didn't live there....

We only lived for a few years at number 223 on 51st Street. We felt we had to move into a better neighborhood. So we moved to number 281 on 51st Street. You know how they say, "In New York you move around the corner and you're in a different world"? We didn't quite make it around the corner. But the move brought us closer to the wealthy Shore Road section and the other expensive-home areas of Brooklyn where I used to wander around hating the people who lived there. At the rate we were moving—about a block every three years—it would have taken us half a century to move into one of those Shore Road homes....

The interesting thing about our new flat was that you could step out of a bedroom window and be on the roof of the tailor shop next door. In summer I used to go out there to practice on my violin. It was a present from my Aunt Marie. Every time the tailor pressed a pair of pants a puff of steam would come sneezing out of a little pipe near where I was playing. That's how I happened to become a hot fiddle player.

Of course, having that roof right next to our window made the place easy to rob. But we didn't worry. Everybody knew

ON CHURCH AVENUE WAS THE FLATBUSH THEATRE A SHOWCASE FOR MANY VAUDE-VILLE ACTS. VAUDEVILLE INSPIRED A GENERATION OF BROOKLYN SONS AND DAUGH-TERS WHO LATER WENT ON TO BECOME STARS IN THEIR OWN RIGHT.

we didn't have anything worth stealing. And Papa was glad for the roof. He was the one who had the idea I should practice out there. He got the idea one evening when my scratching interfered with the sounds of his opera recordings, which he listened to night after night. Come to think of it, I might have been the original Fiddler on the Roof.

I think the people in the neighborhood really loved to hear me play. I know in the winter when it was too cold to go out on the roof and I had to play indoors, the neighborhood kids used to throw stones through the windows just so they could hear me play. My father had great plans for my future. I was to become so good on the violin that I'd play in the orchestra at the Metropolitan Opera. But after listening to me practice for a while, he revised his plans a little. He was willing to settle for the Metropolitan Life. But just to be on the safe side, he said, it would be a good idea, when I got out of grammar school, if I learned a trade. That's the way fathers are. I'm taking an hour violin lesson at a dollar a week, and he's already thrown me out of the pit at the Met....

The first school I went to was P.S. 2 on 45th Street in Brooklyn. I don't remember too much about it because of a game I used to play with some of the other pupils. It was called hooky. This brought me in contact with the principal a lot. He was a man with one arm named Memmot. No. I don't know the name of the other arm. But I do know this: If he'd had two arms and handled me the way he did, I might not have survived.

I really only remember one of the teachers in P.S. 2. His name was Julius Laderberg, and I don't remember him because of anything he contributed to my education. It's because he later went into business with a cousin of mine named Herman Davis. They bought a resort hotel in the Catskills. It was on a pond called Swan Lake, so the genius schoolteacher and my genius cousin, after weeks of thinking, came up with this catchy and creative name for their new hotel ... Swan Lake Inn.

I found Manual Training High much easier than P.S. 2 ...

to get out of. And it looked to me as if they planned it that way. Right in front of the building they had this great big door with the one word ENTRANCE carved above it in stone. But when you get inside, everywhere you looked there were doors with red signs over them that said EXIT. So I did. I must say the school had a fine reputation. Friends of the family were always asking me where I went to school, as if they didn't believe I could get into one. When I told them they'd shake their heads in surprise and say, "You go to Manual Training? Fine school." Then they'd shake their heads some more. Everyone had something good to say about that school except the kids who went there.

There were a lot of *them*. When my class from P.S. 2 got inducted, it brought the number of inmates at Manual Training up to 2,000. Of that number, 1,999 were working to get a diploma and go to college. The other one was working to get out of the building and go to the early show at the Orpheum on Flatbush Avenue.

There were only two things I didn't like about all vaudeville theaters. They had a woman sitting behind a window who sold you a ticket and a man standing in front of the door who wouldn't let you in without it. I'd have seen a lot more vaudeville if it hadn't been for them. I figured those tickets were a big waste. If they'd eliminated the woman who sold them and the man who took them and the cost of printing them, they'd have saved enough money to create scholar-

ships to let students like me in free. I mean students of vaudeville....

Nobody had the idea, yet, of selling all kinds of goodies in the theater lobby. The popcorn machine probably hadn't even been invented. So if a guy expected to spend the whole day seeing a show over and over again (how else can you learn the jokes?), he'd get in early before the prices went up and bring his lunch. I'd buy a corned beef sandwich at Solly's Delicatessen. With the sandwich, just like today, you got garlic pickles free. This was great. The corned beef was nourishment and the pickles guaranteed privacy. There were enough vaudeville theaters around school so that I could go to a different one every day. The Orpheum was the big-time house that changed its bill only once a week. Then there was the Fox, the Flatbush, the Prospect, and a lot of other houses that changed their bill twice, sometimes three times a week. I saw all the great acts of the day like Frank Tinney, Pat Rooney ... Joe Howard, Al Jolson, Finks Mules, and I figured I really belonged in show business when I caught a bill that opened with an act called the Youngman Family. No relation. Can you picture my family walking thirty feet above the floor on a tight wire? But those other Youngmans were wonderful. I guess great talent goes with the name. They did somersaults on the tight wire. That's no trick now, but it was great then. It was doubly great to a kid who couldn't walk a crack on the sidewalk without falling.

The author gratefully acknowledges the use of photographs from the sources listed below. Every attempt was made to trace the proper copyright holders of the photos used herein. Where no credit is given on the celebrity photos indicates use from the celebrity's private collection.

Adams, Joey

Albert, Marv
   Photo: National Broadcasting Company, Inc.

Asimov, Isaac
   Doubleday, Photo: Alex Gotfryd

Auerbach, Red
   Photo: The Boston Celtics

Brody, Jane
   Photo: The New York Times

Califano, Joseph

Carter, Jack

Chisholm, Shirley

Commoner, Barry

Copland, Aaron
   Boosey & Hawkes, Photo: Ralph Titus

Cosell, Howard
   Photo: Capital Cities/ABC, Inc.,

Cypher, Jon

Damone, Vic

Davis, Clive
   Arista Records, Photo: Steve Prezant

Della Femina, Jerry
   Della Femina McNamee, Inc., Photo: Deborah Feingold

Dorfman, Dan
   Photo: USA Today

Edwards, Vince
   Photo: The Greg H. Sims Co.

Gaines, William

Gardenia, Vincent

Ginzburg, Ralph
   Photo: Ralph Ginzburg

Giuliani, Rudolph
   Photo: Anderson, Kill, Olick

& Oshinsky

Gosset, Jr., Louis
   Photo: Dick Zimmerman

Greco, José:
   Photo: Royce Carlton, Inc.

Groh, David
   Photo: Ambrosio/Mortimer & Assoc.

Hackett, Buddy:
   Photo: Hackett Enterprises

Havens, Richie

Holtzman, Elizabeth:
   Office of the Comptroller, The City of New York

Holzman, Red
   Photo: The New York Knicks

Horne, Lena
   Photo: UPI/Bettmann Newsphotos

Ingels, Marty

Jackson, Anne

Kazan, Lainie:
   Photo: Lainie and Company

King, Alan

King, Larry
   Photo: The Larry King Show

Landau, Martin
   Photo: Mike Mamakos & Co

LaRosa, Julius

Manilow, Barry
   Photo: Solters Riskin Friedman

Mazursky, Paul
   Photo: Tecolote Productions

Merrill, Robert
   Photo: General Artists, Inc.

Miller, Arthur
   Photo: UPI Photo

Miller, Henry
   Photo: Bettmann Archives

Modell, Art
   Photo: The Cleveland Browns

Morrow, "Cousin Brucie"
   Photo: WCBS-FM 101.1

Nilsson, Harry
   Photo: AP/Wide World Photo

Paterno, Joe
   Photo: Penn State Football

Rivers, Joan
   Photo: The Joan Rivers Show

Roach, Max
   Photo: SMG Productions

Roker, Jr., Al
   Photo: WNBC-TV, New York

Sarris, Andrew

Schaap, Dick
   Photo: Capital Cities/ABC Inc.

Sedaka, Neil
   Photo: Neil Sedaka Music

Sendak, Maurice
   Photo: Chris Callis

Sills, Beverly
   Photo: Christian Steiner

Silvers, Phil
   Photo: International News Photos

Smits, Jimmy
   Photo: PMK

Snider, Duke
   Photo: UPI/Bettmann Newsphotos

Tooker, George
   Photo: National Academy of Design, New York City

Vereen, Ben

Wallach, Eli
   Photo: Warner Bros. Inc.

West, Mae
   Photo: UPI/Bettmann Newsphotos

Wilkens, Lenny
   Photo: The Cleveland Cavaliers

Youngman, Henny
   Photo: Banner Artists International

ABOUT THE AUTHOR

Ralph Monti is a magazine writer, editor, and publisher who has written
feature articles for a variety of magazines and newspapers. His credits
include features in *The New York Times*, *New York Daily News*,
Newsday, *Christian Science Monitor*, and other award-winning
publications.

He is a native New Yorker who lived in Brooklyn for many years.
While his childhood memories include countless stoopball and empty-
lot baseball games, his big claim to fame was his skill at rescuing
seemingly lost spaldeens that fell to the bottom of sewer drains. If
bubble gum on the top of a stickball bat didn't do the trick, he was the
neighborhood's master at salvaging the ball with a scoop made from an
old clothes hanger. He now lives in New Jersey with his wife, Margaret.